CW00853927

What better way to learn than to see the theme of trust playing out in life's moments. An entertaining, easy to understand and quick way to learn about such a valuable theme in our lives. Lea has very creatively produced a trusted guide for the busy executive.

Andre Misso, VP HR, LTROD, Hong Kong and Shanghai Bank

Lea's message speaks to all of us, whether we are trying to build trust in others or trying to deal with someone who we don't trust. Her characters are believable and her main character redefines how to get ahead in the world. I would recommend this book for anyone who is in the workplace today. An enjoyable read with a powerful message.

Kaye Parker, APR, CHRP, CSP, President, PBBA Atlantic Think Training

Engaging, informative, helpful and entertaining ... A must read for anyone who wants to be successful in a business world where trust is critical but so seldom demonstrated.

Susan Sweeney, CA CSP HoF, President, Connex Network Inc

Trusted: A Leader's Lesson is the fable of a leader who learns the value of trust and in doing so changes his life and his organization's fortunes. An enjoyable read with important insights for business and for life, don't miss it.

Paul J. Zak, Ph.D., Author, The Moral Molecule:
The Source of Love and Prosperity

A compelling read that pulls you in immediately and takes you through a journey of discovery and growth for Hunter, the main character. It is chock full of good, practical advice and leadership lessons that will benefit any reader.

Brent Darnell, Author, The People-Profit Connection

Trust as a leader, follower, friend, father, and spouse are all explored through a story that follows a man through a failure at work and at home to a successful turnaround in life. The theme running throughout the intrigue, suspense, adventure, and romance is trust, trust in the workplace, and trust at home. Lea Brovedani has included in her poignant novel innovative tools such as noble goals, appreciative inquiry, and the Emotion Roadmap™ to help people learn how to build trust in their relationships.

Chuck Wolfe, CEO, Charles J. Wolfe Associates

TRUSTED

A LEADER'S LESSON

LEA BROVEDANI

EMOTIONAL INTELLIGENCE PRESS

TRUSTED: A Leader's Lesson

© 2013 Lea Brovedani

ALL RIGHTS RESERVED

No part of this publication may be reproduced or distributed in any form or by any means, or stored in a database or retrieval system, without the prior written permission of the publisher.

Six Seconds Emotional Intelligence Press
San Francisco, California
www.6seconds.org/tools

ISBN: 978-1-935667-17-9

Library of Congress Control Number: 2013933563

Printed and bound in the United States

Interior Layouts: Sushil Kumar,
AG Creative Solutions, New Delhi
email: agcreativesolutions@gmail.com

TABLE OF CONTENTS

To the fates,
who showed me what love looked like
and let me marry him
and to the children that resulted.

Hunter tried to swallow but there was no spit to moisten his throat and his lips kept sticking to his teeth. His mouth felt like an Indian dirt road before the monsoons. The coins in his pocket jingled from the tremors that shook his legs.

Standing backstage at the Community Heroes awards, waiting for his name to be called, he wondered why he felt this way.

Sure, he'd talked to big crowds before. As a CEO he'd impressed buyers by his stage presence. But this was different. Somehow it just mattered more – this time is was just him speaking from the heart and hoping his words would show his gratitude.

In his wildest dreams he never imagined speaking at something like this. The Community Heroes Award. How did he get here?

No one, not even Hunter, could have predicted the path his life had taken over the past five years. Once a successful entrepreneur, he never imagined he could lose his company, or have to start over again, but then he doubted few businessmen anticipate such an outcome.

His mind wandered back to his old business, Birkett Canopy and Lounge Furniture, which was considered the Cadillac of lawn furniture. Originally his uncle's business, Hunter took it over to keep it in the family. He had started with a solid business plan and team, and all indications suggested a promising future. Yet what should have been a family legacy spanning generations ended with him.

All that was left at the end of the two years Hunter ran the company was a drawer full of unpaid bills and considerable heartache. He was glad his uncle wasn't alive to see what had happened.

He knew why the business failed.

It failed when he lived in that place of not trusting himself or others – a place of doubt, fear, and anger. During that time, he didn't grow, and he knew he didn't make good decisions. He bought new equipment and borrowed against future profits.

As profits dropped, he got more reactive, more impatient – and more afraid.

Scared and feeling responsible for the future of the company he started looking for a 'magic bullet'. A cure that would solve all of the problems in the company that he didn't feel qualified to manage. The bullet came in the form of "the perfect" business deal, and it killed his company.

His throat tightened when he thought of the friendships he had lost. "Let it go, Hunter," he said to himself. An announcement on stage brought him back to the present moment. He grabbed the curtain and peeked out into the audience.

In the front row, he could see his daughter sitting next to his new wife. Their close bond pleased him. "So this is what happy feels like," he thought. He looked around trying to take in all of the images and smells. "I never want to forget these moments, or take them for granted." The words he had to say came back to him, and they were strong and honest. The shaking stopped.

Hunter could also see his close friend Rick Phillips, talking to his ex boss and mentor, Susan Cannon. He remembered a time when he felt like no one was in his corner. Now he was receiving an award that demonstrated the positive impact he had on the lives of others. It meant a lot to have his friends here. Susan was one of the main reasons he was here tonight, and he knew she would be embarrassed when he dedicated the award to her. He had talked it over with his wife, A.J., and she was in complete agreement because, if not for Susan, he wouldn't be where he was.

The thought of receiving the Community Heroes humanitarian award continued to stir up memories from the last five years of his life. In that time, he went from broke and feeling busted in spirit to living a rich and full life. It hadn't been easy to climb back up from losing his company, or his first marriage. Staying down would have been easier, but he knew it was an awful place to live.

He looked out at the scene in front of him and his gaze took in everything and nothing.

While he knew he'd changed, it was all too easy to remember the disaster he'd left behind.

CHAPTER 1

BROKE AND BUSTED – DEFINING TRUST

Hunter had started working for his uncle's company when he was a teenager in university. His uncle thought it was the best way to groom him for the management team. From a stock boy sending out shipments of lawn furniture, to building the sets, to the head of marketing, Hunter steadily moved up the corporate ladder taking control of the company sooner than he was ready when his uncle died of a heart attack.

He wasn't ready to lead but he jumped in head first, knowing that if he didn't, the company would cease to exist. Not only did he know everyone in the company on a first-name basis, Hunter knew their kids' names and how much they owed on their houses. He took the close relationships for granted. He didn't realize they were very important to him until they were gone, along with the business.

When Hunter declared bankruptcy it wasn't only the business that he lost. His marriage to Ellen had ended because she said she was tired of listening to his anger. It particularly hurt Hunter when Ellen said his daughter wouldn't miss him because she hardly knew him.

He hadn't just wanted to run Birkett Lounge and Canopy, he had wanted to grow it and make it an international star. He had never thought small and his big dreams became a nightmare. He felt alone and afraid, and hated that feeling so much that he channeled it into anger.

"It was because of that young hot shot," Hunter said to convince himself. He recalled the meeting that was the catalyst for his current situation as if it were yesterday. Hunter was sitting in his office analyzing the company's first-quarter earnings. He knew that, unless a large order came in, the company would be in big trouble.

The new machinery he had insisted on to expand the product line had maxed out the corporate credit line, and Hunter wasn't certain he could meet the payroll for the month. So engrossed was he in the figures that Hunter barely glanced up when Ed Southern, a lawyer representing the retail giant Mallco, walked into his office.

The young lawyer's stammer caught Hunter's attention. "Mr. Birkett? M-M-Mr. Birkett? I'm E-E – Ed Southern, a lawyer from Mallco, and I-I-I'm here to inquire about the production of your Birkett Kids' Canopy and Lounger set, which has been b-b-brought to our attention. We want to order one hundred and fifty thousand units."

Now he had Hunter's undivided attention. A miniature version of the company's bestseller, the kids' set had been created for a promotional event. Hunter knew the machines in the shop weren't specifically set up to produce this version, and time and cost meant they hadn't made more than three hundred to date, but it had been a huge success in terms of the attention and buzz it generated. Now, here was a guy from Mallco, with a contract worth an obscene amount of money, asking Hunter to produce one hundred and fifty thousand of them. The number boggled his mind.

Even so, Hunter knew it would be a challenge to meet such an order, so he made a counter pitch. "Well, if you like the kids' set, you're going to love our adult line. In fact, we can produce our Deluxe Canopy and Lounger for less than the cost of the kids' set."

But Ed held firm. "Sorry, M-M-Mr. Birkett, we have l-l-l-lots of adult models, what we p-p-particularly liked about your k-kids' set was the q-q-quality of the p-product. We know p-parents will want it. If you're not able to b-build it, I understand and I w-won't take up anymore of your time."

The young lawyer made a move to stand up, and Hunter thought he saw a slight smile on his face. Was this multi-million dollar opportunity about to walk out the door? He wasn't sure. Hunter knew from his business colleagues that if you said no to Mallco once, you usually didn't get a second chance and the threat of not making payroll played on his mind. He had never planned to manufacture kids' furniture, but he needed the money to keep the company going.

For a moment, Hunter thought about bringing in his senior managers to discuss the pros and cons, but the lawyer seemed ready to walk and he was afraid of losing the deal. Hunter silently studied Ed Southern. He was close to six feet tall and couldn't have weighed more than one hundred and fifty pounds. His Adam's apple seemed to bob up and down above his too big shirt collar. The suit looked like an expensive custom tailored job, but it made him look even younger since it was in such contrast to his youthful awkwardness.

As Hunter continued to stare at him, Ed's glasses slid down his nose. He used his middle finger to push them back in place and he swung side to side in his chair.

In that moment, Hunter made a fateful decision; he would sign the contract. He felt the weight of his responsibility to the people in the company and didn't trust that he could keep the company afloat without this deal. His employees would be safe and he envisioned the looks on their faces when they saw the bonus on their paychecks!

"This kid is no match for me!" thought Hunter. "I can definitely out maneuver this naïve, stuttering young lawyer."

If Hunter had done his homework, he would have known that Ed Southern was one of Mallco's top contract lawyers, and he used other people's perceptions about his appearance and stammer to his advantage. But Hunter saw only inexperience and naiveté, and he believed he could use those to his advantage. It was one of many bad decisions he would later regret.

"Give me the contract, Ed, and let me have a look." Hunter read it over, smiled, and said, "It looks like I'm in the kids' furniture business!"

"M-M-Mr. Birkett, we can give you a w-week to have your lawyers look over the contract before you sign." But Hunter had his pen in hand. With considerable bravado, he signed the contract and stood up to shake hands with Ed.

"Listen kid," Hunter said, smiling. "If you have a good brain, you don't need a lawyer."

Hunter left early that day. His mind was focused on how to tell his management team about the new contract. The bravado he felt in his office had given way to serious misgivings, and Hunter wondered if he should have waited until his senior management team weighed in before signing on the dotted line.

"Too late now," he thought to himself, "we'll find a way to make it work".

The headache had started when he left the office and the sleepless night had made it even worse. At 6:30 a.m., he decided to head into the office and go over what he was going to say to them. He had finished his second pot of coffee when staff started to arrive.

He ushered his senior team into the room. There was the VP of Finance, the Head of Production, the new Marketing Manager, and the head of the design team, Rick Phillips. Rick was a mechanical engineer and Hunter's best friend. They had gone through school together, served as best man at each other's weddings and Hunter knew that he could trust Rick with anything.

Rick and Hunter met in university when they shared a room. Rick's nickname was Bait, for his ability to attract women. He seemed oblivious to his own good looks and he had a spark and intelligence that made people want to be with him. He was also Hunter's wingman and there were many nights of romance that Hunter could thank Rick for.

After Rick completed his degree in mechanical engineering, he worked at a few small manufacturing companies before Hunter convinced him to work for Birkett Canopy. They had made a great team, Hunter was the idea guy and Rick would make it happen. Hunter loved the man like a brother.

Seeing the quizzical looks at the impromptu meeting, Hunter made his announcement.

"Great news everyone! Get ready to celebrate because we've got an order from Mallco that is going to knock your socks off!"

The team broke out into whoops and hollers, and started high fiving each other. For a moment, Hunter immersed himself in the warm feeling of their approval.

Hunter explained that the contract was forone hundred and fifty thousand kids' units. Suddenly, it was as if someone had hit the mute button. They looked at Hunter with disbelief.

Rick broke the silence. "You're joking, right? You do know that the kids' set took twice as long to make, at twice the cost of our adult set?"

Hunter's accountant chimed in, noting the company barely broke even producing a few hundred kids' sets, so how the hell did Hunter expect that the same expenses times one hundred and fifty thousand would produce different results?

The kicker came when someone asked, "OK, let's look it over and see if there is anything we can work with. How much time do we have before you have to sign?"

Hunter was silent and looked down at his sweating palms, thinking of how to tell them, but his silence told them the answer.

The signed contract came out, and that's when Hunter's life started to go downhill. For the next six months, he pushed, cajoled, and pleaded with his staff to meet the requirements of the order. He became a man possessed, working fourteen hour days, six days a week. On his one day off, he slept and his family and friendships suffered. All regular production was put aside and longstanding clients turned to other vendors. Rick, tired of the long hours, lack of appreciation, and the fact Hunter constantly turned him away when he wanted to discuss the situation, left the company.

It was a low point for Hunter, who felt he had lost both his best friend and one of his best employees. Without Rick's expertise, it proved impossible to adapt the complex manufacturing equipment to produce the kids' sets more rapidly and economically, and the company starting breaking down. Deadlines were missed and Mallco, citing a clause in the contract, began to levy fines. Hunter started riding everyone in the company to work overtime and, one by one, his top people defected. Eventually, the fines from missed deadlines made it impossible to make a profit.

Less than a year from signing the contract, Hunter realized the company was bleeding and there was no way he could keep it going. He had started to invest the family savings, but that exacerbated problems that already existed in his own marriage. His wife asked for a divorce.

There was no choice, he had to find investors or declare bankruptcy. "Who is going to invest in a company that loses more money than it makes?" Hunter asked himself. The long hours and constant stress had taken their toll and he made the difficult decision to declare bankruptcy. After Hunter signed the final papers with the lawyer's, he walked away with nothing more than a few pieces of good lawn furniture to show for the five years that he ran the company.

In that last year, Hunter put on forty pounds. A steady diet of coffee and fast food during the day and scotch at night had aged him five years. Before he declared bankruptcy, he sat down with each of his employees and apologized. He found the yelling easier to take than the tears, and he was sure they all hated him for the demise of the company. The weight of his heart grew with each one he told.

He was appreciative and humbled when one of them recommended him for a position and now he was about to start a job with a large company called Fixtures. For the first time ever, Hunter would be working for strangers. He signed the contract at 2:00 p.m. on Thursday with a start date of the following Monday.

Rather than go home to an empty apartment, Hunter stopped at his favorite pub. At 10:00 p.m., he was still sitting there, his shirt un-tucked and his hair hanging over one eye.

Hunter felt the indentation on the finger of his left hand where his wedding ring had been. "Damn it!" he muttered louder then he intended. He checked his wallet, pulled out his last bills, and put up his hand to order a row of drinks.

He thought about the last six months and downed one. "Damn it!" he said again. He shot back another and slammed the empty glass on the table. "Lucky to ave a job! Ha!" Hunter's look of pain returned.

"Yersh of seventy hour weeks. Yersh of hardly drawing a pay-sheck," Hunter slurred. "Yersh of puttin' the compny before anythin and everthing, and being left with nothin'! Lucky!" What pained him the most was the knowledge that it all could have been avoided. "All gone because I trushed too much," he slurred aloud, trying to convince himself more than anyone.

The people at the next table gave him a strange look.

"To think I was taken in by that damned kid," Hunter muttered. It felt good to focus the anger on someone other than himself.

In his drunken state he cursed at the world, blaming anyone and everyone but himself for the downfall of his company. He thought of the comment from the lawyers, as he signed the final papers closing his company, that he was lucky to have found a job. He laughed aloud. To no one in particular, he raised his glass and yelled, "Cheersh! Here's to one damn lucky guy!"

The people at the table next to him moved away.

FIRST WEEK ON THE NEW JOB

Hunter sat at his new desk. "This is where I was twenty years ago," he thought to himself, "working as the marketing guy."

He smiled, remembering the first sign he had when he started working after he graduated from University. His uncle had written it with colored marker on a piece of paper and stuck it to the door on the broom closet they called his office.

"Manager of WTFK Division" His uncle was fond of telling people that it stood for "Who the #@?% Knows." It was crude, but he knew his uncle was proud of him even though he didn't really understand what he did.

The sign on his desk this time was made of brass and said "VP of Marketing – Faucets". The sign cost more than his first day of wages at his old company. Working for Fixtures, one of North America's largest most successful manufacturers of faucets and drains wasn't originally what Hunter had in mind. There was a certain irony to it, given that his business had washed down the drain.

He looked around and everyone seemed cheerful. It seemed that everyone who walked by his office took a moment to stop and wish him well in his new role. "Great," he muttered. "Just what I need. Now I'll be expected to smile like an idiot when they walk by and say 'good morning.'" Hunter hated his life. He thought it would make a great country and western song: My Business is Gone, My Wife Left me and the Dog up and Died. All true, except he didn't have a dog.

He was sitting in his pool of pity when his boss, Susan Cannon, Executive Vice President of Sales and marketing, walked by.

"Hi Hunter! Hope you're settling in okay. It's so great to have you onboard."

"I'm doing great, thanks," he responded.

"Good, good. Do you have a couple minutes?"

"Sure," he said.

"We haven't had a chance to formally meet since you joined the team," Susan said, smiling warmly.

Susan was barely over five feet but her presence and confidence made her seem taller. Her hair and nails were always impeccably done and her clothes appeared unwrinkled even at the end of the day.

Susan was a woman who got things done. With a combined background in psychology and finance, she wasn't easily defined, and her strong ethics and ability to see outside the box made her both an asset and a liability to the company. She had been known on occasion to butt heads with senior managers for her unwillingness to compromise on issues that she felt went against her values and beliefs.

In fact, rumor had it that, in her interview with the president, Susan said, "Don't expect me to leave my humanity at the door for the sake of profit." It was a credit to the president and his organization that they hired her regardless, knowing that she would challenge them on humanity issues on a regular basis. These issues ranged from canceling contracts for products made in countries that didn't recognize child labor laws to determining the appropriate steps to take when an employee wasn't working out as a team player.

Susan's reputation as someone who could be trusted was so strong that it extended to the companies she worked for. That alone was worth more than its weight in gold.

When Hunter walked in the door of Susan's office, he noticed a sign on her desk. It read:

> **Trust:**
>
> **The willingness to accept vulnerability based upon positive expectations about another's behavior.[1]**

Hunter said, "Trusting the wrong people cost me my business." The words came out before he had a chance to think about what he was saying.

Susan gave Hunter a look that was both compassionate and perceptive. "Explain what you mean." Susan sat down and motioned for Hunter to sit.

Hunter found himself recounting what had happened to him. He told her about the people he had worked with, and how much he cared for and missed them. He admitted he was hurt, since they talked to him as if he was the bad guy and acted like they didn't trust him. Although he revealed more than he had intended, there was something about the way she listened without judgement, or interrupting, that made him feel safe.

When he was done, Susan said, "I believe that we are given a lot of lessons in life, and the hardest ones have the biggest returns." She smiled and added, "It seems like you're ready for a big return. I like to know the people who work for me. You got a few minutes just to talk?"

---

1 Jennifer Dunn and Maurice Sweitzer

She turned and looked at the definition of trust that sat on her desk and turned to look at Hunter. "What is your definition of trust?"

At first, Hunter thought Susan was being condescending. But when he looked at her, he realized she was serious, and really interested in what he had to say.

All this talk was starting to make Hunter really uncomfortable and he leaned back in his chair. Now he was regretting spilling his guts, convinced he had given her way too much personal information. "Trust? Well it means that someone is honest with you. It means that they won't cheat you. Ah, I don't know, it means that they've got integrity!"

Susan nodded. "I agree with all of that, and I'll add something. Trust starts with you. In order to trust others, you have to trust yourself first. To do that, you need to know yourself. "Susan realized Hunter was uncomfortable by the way he kept shifting his glance and moving in his seat, so she decided to change the topic to ease Hunter's discomfort. "OK, enough of waxing philosophically for the moment. Let's get down to business. Let's look at what you need to concentrate on from a business perspective. We've set some pretty aggressive targets for you to reach, and I've heard you're the guy to trust to get it done."

Hunter's body relaxed. He was happy to get away from the talk about personal things and he was in his element now. He loved marketing and caught himself laughing and smiling as he went over the details of the new job and the challenges he would face. Susan asked him tough questions and for a few minutes they verbally sparred over marketing direction. Susan spoke her mind and expected those who worked for her to do the same. He felt encouraged to know he wouldn't be expected to keep quiet when he disagreed and she genuinely seemed to want his differing opinion. The deep furrows in his forehead softened and he caught himself smiling.

He felt a huge sense of relief, one he hadn't felt during the five years he had run his own company – a company that had cost him his marriage and some great friends. He realized he hadn't been able to do what he loved, and had spent most of his time in administrative work, which he hated. He caught a glimmer of his old self and it felt good.

THE EMAIL

The first email Hunter saw in his inbox after his meeting with Susan asked him about his personal development plan. He didn't feel he needed one and was quite certain he could do an effective job without any of that soft stuff. It was one of the things he was told was different about this company – they really invested in their people. If he had his way, the company would invest in stock options for him and he'd reap the rewards, keeping his nose down and doing his job in the meantime.

He recalled the battery of tests he did when he came on board. These included an emotional intelligence assessment that measured his abilities and competency in the personal, emotional and social skills needed to cope with the demands and pressures of life. He also did a personality assessment, a communications assessment, and a values and ethics assessment. He was wondering when they were going to assess his table manners. Hunter thought it was a waste of money.

What Hunter didn't know was that Susan had hired him against the advice of the Human Resource manager, who believed his lower emotional intelligence score in self-awareness could pose a problem. During the interview, Susan saw a lot of promise and po-tential, and her gut told her that Hunter was worth the risk. She also knew that the scores may have been lower than his actual abilities, given what he had been through over the past year. When he talked about things he loved in his business, she saw considerable warmth for the people he worked with, one that belied his low interpersonal skills score.

Regardless, Hunter's high scores in other areas, not to mention his engaging and outgoing personality, helped compensate for any deficiencies and she knew Hunter had to work on these areas if he was going to excel at Fixtures. The first step, it seemed to her, was getting Hunter to be more self-aware.

Susan sent Hunter an email asking him to read over the infor-mation on his Johari window.

He saw the URGENT icon when the email was delivered to his inbox and decided to ignore it.

"Crap!" Hunter muttered under his breath. "What's so urgent about this stuff? All this talk from Susan about feelings! She's my boss, not my shrink. Just tell me what needs done and I'll do it. I don't need to talk about my friggin feelings!" He was glad he was alone since the scowl on his face said it all.

The information on the front page told Hunter the Johari Window had been developed in the early 1950s by two psychologists — Joe Luft and Harry Ingraham. Hunt and Ingraham realized there are certain things we know about ourselves, and others that we don't. Similarly, there are certain things others know about us that we may not be aware of. It takes energy to hide information from ourselves and from others, and the more information we know, the better and clearer we know ourselves, and how we communicate with others.

Hunter knew this to be true, since there were times when he had worked hard at pretending everything was OK in his business. He found out later that he hadn't fooled anyone, and the energy he had spent keeping up the lie cost him friendships, his marriage and his peace of mind.

He almost felt like scrapping the job opportunity since the whole process made him feel ridiculous. It reminded him of the letter he had sent to a girl in Grade Four. Do you like me Yes____ No____. Will you go to the dance with me Yes___ No____. "Ridiculous crap," Hunter muttered to himself.

Hunter was frowning and trying to make sense of his Johari Window when Susan walked into his office.

"Hunter, don't look so miserable," Susan said.

Hunter scowled.

She couldn't decide whether he looked confused or distraught, so began to explain the tool. "It's a simple way to get to know yourself better."

"I'm not sure I WANT to know myself better. Haven't you heard, ignorance is bliss." The words were supposed to be funny, but he couldn't keep the annoyance out of his voice.

Susan knew that there was a lot to learn and explore with him. When she'd hired Hunter, HR had him take assessments that included feedback from others. There were still a few people from his old company who were still speaking to him, so he asked them. Unfortunately, a lot of the comments focused on his weaknesses. Reading their comments Hunter first felt a flash of anger and then sadness. The thought that people he had worked with and cared for did not see him as caring or trustworthy made him feel like a loser.

"So, Hunter," said Susan, "what did you think when you looked over your report? Were there any surprises?"

Hunter replied, "It seems like I have the profile of Jabba the Hutt! No one sees me as caring, trustworthy, or dependable."

"Come on, it's not that bad," Susan countered. "I received a copy as well, and it looks like you're focusing on the negative here. You're also seen as friendly, helpful, intelligent, proud and powerful. That's something to feel good about!"

"But I'm not sure why they don't trust me." Hunter said quietly.

Susan leaned forward, "Trust is one of my core values. Now if we are going to work together, I have to trust you, and I believe I can otherwise I wouldn't have hired you."

She glanced down at her notes, "I'd like to know why some of your colleagues don't see you as trustworthy even though you have also listed it as one of your core values." Susan softened her harsh words with a quiet smile.

A flash of anger showed on Hunter's face but was almost instantly replaced by a look of guilt and remorse.

"I expect you're interested in finding out as well, aren't you?" she asked.

Hunter could feel last night's dinner turn in his stomach. What could he say? He was afraid to find out why people he cared for didn't trust him, but this was a new boss, and he needed the job, so he said the only thing he felt he could say, "Sure."

Misery moved in like a broke relative with no conscience.

Susan smiled, knowing that his "sure" was forced. She also knew Hunter had to be able to handle the position and he needed to develop his emotional intelligence skills. Her training told her that she needed to make him a little uncomfortable in order for him to start the change process. She would provide support while he went through the process,and would hope that the investment would pay off.

THE CALL ON THE CON

At that moment, Susan got a call on her cell phone. She looked at Hunter and said, "Sorry, I have to take this," and walked off to her office. The call was from her father, Harry, who sounded both excited and agitated. Once the owner of a successful contracting company, he was in the first stages of Alzheimer's . He would often call Susan four times in a row, asking the same question. She had wanted him to move in with her or get a companion to come in on a day to day basis but he refused to give up his independence. Susan knew she would have to insist on it eventually and it broke her heart to think about it. It was a struggle for her; she wanted to remember him as the guy that could solve and do anything. He had, after all, stayed with her mother, taking care of her until an addiction to alcohol took her life. Susan's strong personality and character came from him, and she knew that he hated being dependent on her. And she hated watching as Alzheimer's slowly claimed the father she knew.

"Hey, Susiecue. Exciting times. Exciting times. Your ole man is going undercover. I need you to bring me a thousand bucks in small bills for a sting operation. I was told not to tell anyone, but I know you can keep a secret. A man from the bank called me and said that I could be a secret police man and help him catch a thief. I need to give him a thousand bucks, but he promised he'd give it back to me tomorrow." Harry sounded elated.

"What!? Listen, Dad, don't do anything! I'll be right there and you can explain it all to me then. OK?" Susan could hear her voice rise and tried to keep the panic at bay.

"You sound mad, Susie." Harry sounded like a young child who had been caught stealing a cookie.

"No, I'm not mad. Listen, why don't you put on that movie that you like.

"The Holy Grail? I love that movie." Harry chuckled.

"Yeah... Monty Python. I'll be there before it's over."

"OK. Don't forget the cash." Harry hung up the phone.

With that she grabbed her coat and purse and burst out of her office.

Hunter saw Susan talking to her assistant and could hear the urgent staccato of her voice rise and fall. He had thought for sure that he was witnessing an employee getting yelled at until the assistant jumped up and gave Susan a quick hug.

Susan swept by Hunter with a look of alarm and anger on her face.

"Man, she must be one heck of a boss if she can yell at an employee and get a hug in return," Hunter thought.

At 11:15 a.m. he walked over to Milly, Susan's assistant, and said, "I was supposed to have a meeting with Susan at 11:00 a.m. Do you know if she'll be back soon or should I reschedule?"

"I'll reschedule you for tomorrow, Hunter. Ms. Cannon might not be back today." Milly opened up the schedule on her computer. "She can see you tomorrow at 11:00 a.m. Is that good for you?"

"Yeah... that works. By the way. What's up? The boss looked a little miffed." Hunter leaned against the desk and smiled.

"A personal matter," Milly said with a smile that told Hunter not to ask any more questions.

Susan let herself into Harry's apartment. She could hear the television blaring and him laughing.

When she walked in, he hit the pause button and looked up at her. "Hey Susiecue, what are you doing here in the middle of the day?"

Susan leaned down and gave Harry a kiss on the cheek. "We talked about a bank inspector calling you this morning, Dad. I wanted to hear more."

For a moment Harry looked confused, but then he responded with an annoyed tone, "I haven't completely lost it. I remember. Yer right, the bank inspector called and wants me to help them find a crook."

"What was the bank inspectors name, Dad?"

"Wait a minute, I got it right here." Harry picked up the book that Susan had given him. When he started forgetting things, Susan convinced him to write everything down in a book. Now Harry kept it close and wrote down everything.

"His name is Mr. Smith. He picked me because he needs the help of an honest citizen." Harry beamed. "He's legit, Susie. I made sure of it. He knew everything about me and my bank accounts."

Susan looked down and saw a credit card bill and utility bills sitting in the garbage can. She had asked Harry to shred everything before throwing them away but it was obvious that he had forgotten. One more thing that she would have to be vigilant about.

Susan closed her eyes. "OK Dad. I'm going to call the bank manager and talk to him."

"No!" Harry yelled, startling Susan. He started to get agitated.

Fumbling through the book he came to a page and poked it with his finger. "You can't do that, Susie. Mr. Smith said the bank manager might be in on it."

Even three months prior Harry wouldn't have fallen for this. Now she had to figure out a way to protect him without destroying his dignity.

Susan was quiet for a few minutes while she worked things out. "Dad, I have to be back at my office for a meeting, but how about if you come with me. I could use your advice on a project I'm working on. You can look it over while I go to my meeting." Susan was afraid to leave Harry by himself and knew that asking for his help was the easiest way to get him to come with her.

When they got back to the office, Susan took Harry to the empty board room. She went and pulled out an old project and took it and a cup of coffee to him. She knew that it would keep Harry occupied for awhile. "Read this over and let me know if you think we should go ahead with the deal."

She walked towards her office and stopped to talk to Milly, "See if you can find a number for someone in the police department who deals with fraud. Harry's been targeted and I need to get this taken care of without letting him know. He's convinced that this 'bank inspector' is a good guy and nothing I can say will change that." She didn't see Hunter until it was too late.

Hunter looked embarrassed and started to walk away. He paused, stopped and turned around and said, "I'm sorry, I didn't mean to eavesdrop. Is Harry the older gentleman I saw you with?"

"Yes. He's my Dad."

Hunter said, "Do you mind if I ask if the con's already happened?"

"No. The slime has been working on my Dad to gain his confidence. He has Alzheimer's, so he's an easy target," explained Susan.

Hunter gave Susan a look of sympathetic concern. "I know old folks who have lost thousands of dollars and wouldn't report it because they were embarrassed. I have a friend in the fraud squad at the police department. I'm sure he could help. Would you like me to give him a call?"

Susan looked at Hunter, paused, and opened the door to her office. Although she was always in control in the workplace, she often felt overwhelmed when it came to her family life, and was happy that she had someone who could help.

Hunter called Inspector Perrin to explain what had happened, putting the call on speakerphone so Susan could hear the conversation and add any details that he might have missed. After listening to the story, Inspector Perrin explained that since no money had been taken, no crime had occurred. The only way to prosecute was to catch the crook in the act.

"These are first rate a-holes who prey on seniors or sad lonely people. You might already know this, but the term con man is short for confidence man. They make people believe that they can be confident enough to trust them with their money. But the more people know about this, the harder it is for them to pull it off. We could try to catch him if Harry was up to being bait," said Inspector Perrin. His voice sounded weary.

Susan shook her head. "There's no way. I'm sorry. My Dad has Alzheimer's and it just wouldn't work. I just want to make sure he's safe."

"I'm sorry then. There isn't much we can do. I know it's not what you want to hear. Just be glad that he didn't get any money from your father." Inspector Perrin continued, "I'll send you a list of websites that give you tips to avoid being conned. The basic rule is if someone tells you something that sounds too good to be true, or if you aren't sure, get them to give you references. If it is legitimate, they won't mind if you ask. If they start trying to intimidate you, or get angry that you are questioning them, walk away."

"That's it? We let this creep continue to target old people? And what about Harry? When this guy calls again, Harry will do whatever he says!" There were bright red spots on Susan's cheeks. If Hunter had known her longer he would have been shocked to see her so rattled. Susan was the person who kept her calm in board meetings when everyone else was losing theirs.

Hunter spoke up, "Bill, would you be able to talk to Harry? Tell him that you're leading the division and you have a message for Mr. Smith who is deep undercover."

"Let me check my schedule." There was a long pause. "Where is Harry right now? I've got some time free this morning."

While Susan and Hunter waited for Inspector Perrin to show up Susan talked about Harry. Hunter learned things he never would have under normal situations.

Once he showed up, the three of them brainstormed and came up with a story that Harry would accept. Inspector Perrin would meet Harry in the board room. A carefully worded message would be given to him to pass on to 'Bank Inspector Smith'.

The message read,

Crook has been identified. Inspector Perrin of Division Fifteen is in pursuit. Call off sting.

After the morning with Inspector Perrin, Hunter and Susan realized a new understanding and relationship was starting to develop. A new trust was being established and it felt good.

On the way home Hunter thought about the day. He thought of what his friend had said about old or sad lonely people being the easiest to target. He decided to skip his usual stop at the bar and head straight home. He took the stairs up to his apartment. Some soul searching was in order.

CHAPTER 2

FINDING THE VALUE – EMOTIONS AND EMOTIONAL INTELLIGENCE

H unter had been on the job for three months. It was a common sight to see him at his desk before anyone else arrived in the morning and still be there working when the cleaning staff was sweeping up the flotsam of the day. Like a Hollywood child star, he wanted to prove he still had what it takes. He was pleasant with everyone and worked hard, but he kept his distance. No one knew anything about him – except some delicious rumors.

Some said he was a pathetic chump who had been taken advantage of by a mega corporation... others that he was an amazing swindler who had hidden millions and was working at Fixtures until the heat died down. One rumor said he had snorted up all of the Birkett company profits and had done a stint in rehab. That piece of gossip had taken a life of its own. Supposedly it had all been filmed and they would be viewing it on cable TV in the spring.

Hunter was oblivious. After the pain of losing Birkett Canopy, he just wanted to do his work. But he came across as a black hole, telling others nothing about himself and asking nothing personal about them. In the absence of solid information, people filled the void with a lot of hot air. The pin in the rumor balloon was Susan Cannon's trust in him.

He was efficient and polite to everyone, but his staff stopped talking when he approached, unsure of how to act around him. He spent the good part of each day tracking down information he needed since he missed the small talk that would have given him much of what he needed to know. Projects moved slowly since no one offered up information. Much of his time was spent reacting to problems that needed to be fixed and it frustrated him since most of them could have been avoided.

One early morning, Hunter's mind was preoccupied with reading emails on his phone and not on the signs surrounding the new sidewalk in front of the office. He was deep in thought on what he needed to do and say to get his team together; otherwise, he would have heard the yells of the construction worker and stopped.

"Hey, stop, don't step on that... the cement is wet... don't step there, don't step there. OH CRAP!"

Hunter looked up when he heard the profanity but it was too late, his foot was in mid air and he couldn't stop the momentum before he stepped firmly in the middle of the newly poured sidewalk. He could feel the weight of the cement close in around his shoe and past his ankle in a wet oozing mass. He tried to pull his foot out, but with one foot inside the cement and one outside, he was having difficulty. The harder he tried the more it looked like he was going to lose his balance completely and do a complete face plant in the wet concrete. He tried balancing his briefcase with his computer above his head while leaning backward to pull out the foot inside the cement when the ridiculousness of the situation hit him and he started to laugh.

There he was, full stride, one foot in the cement and one on the road. He looked up and saw he was the center of attention. He recognized a couple of people who reported to him, and they were doing their best not to laugh. The effort was causing their faces to contort in what looked like pain. The construction worker who moments before had been swearing at him, also started to laugh, and pretty soon Hunter had a crowd of people surrounding him and everyone was doubled over with laughter.

With tears of laughter streaming down his face he finally managed to say, "Could someone help pull me out of here before it completely dries and I'm a permanent fixture at Fixtures." Caught up in the moment of common camaraderie, everyone howled with laughter.

One person grabbed Hunter's briefcase and phone so he could get his balance and then a tug of war was waged against the cement and he was pulled free. Unfortunately for Hunter, the weight of the cement pulled off his shoe and the wet cement closed and pooled around it as soon as he removed his foot. He was a sight to behold. One shoeless foot and part of his leg were encased in wet cement, making it look like he was wearing a thick grey boot. Fortunately, the construction worker came over with his dowel and scraped off as much as he could, chuckling the whole while, knowing that the drying cement weighed a lot and because of its quick drying properties would have given Hunter a solid boot in less than an hour. He didn't even seem to mind repairing the spot that Hunter had ruined.

Hunter heard a voice from the crowd. "Mr. Birkett, I've got my sports bag here and we look about the same size. If you want you can have my track suit and running shoes." An employee working under contract for Fixtures made the offer. With one shoe on and the other foot still covered in cement, Hunter was grateful for the offer and was working hard to get some semblance of dignity back.

"Thank you. I'll return it as soon as I can." He made it up the stairs to the front entrance but not without stares and quiet laughter following him.

Hunter could see the tracks that he was leaving on the floor leading into the locker room and reminded himself to apologize to the cleaning staff. He tried hopping on the one shoed foot but the cement still clinging to his pants fell off in clumps and the effort made him out of breath. "Whoa, Hunter," he said to himself, "time to get back in shape. This is pathetic."

After his shower he looked around for a towel and when he couldn't find one grabbed his shirt and dried off. When he was done, he rolled up the suit and wet shirt into a ball and pulled out the track suit from the gym bag. The track suit was a size too small and looked like tights on him, and the running shoes pinched his feet. Hunter knew that he had to wear this or put the cement covered pants and one shoe back on. He went with the tight track suit. When he looked in the mirror he thought he looked like a bad lounge act from the 70's.

"Well," Hunter thought, "It's still pretty early, maybe I can sneak through the office without anyone seeing me and I'll dash home and change before anyone else notices." Fat chance! Forty minutes had passed since his foot landed in the cement and everyone was at work. The news had spread, and when he walked out of the locker room, a few people were waiting for him. As he walked down the hall, a couple of them stood up and started to clap. Hunter laughed, made a couple of bows and exited for the door.

Hunter managed to make it home, get changed and get back to the office in an hour, but it meant he was late for his early morning meeting with Susan. When he walked back into the office he thought that Susan had missed the news about his morning escapade because she didn't laugh or chuckle when he walked into her office. With a perfect poker face she said, "Hunter, I'm all for you making your mark with the company but you have to watch where you're going so you don't overstep your bounds." She paused before adding "Next time, it might be better to leave a paper trail rather than a cement trail," and she started to laugh.

Hunter blushed and responded, "Yeah, it was pretty funny. Now I just have to figure out how to get my dignity back so people will respect and trust that I can manage my department."

"It's a good bunch here, Hunter," Susan said "From what I've studied, I know that positive feelings are linked to trust. People were unsure about you. Now that people here see a more friendly fun side of you, I'm sure you'll find them opening up more."

"So what are you saying, Susan? Are you saying people will trust me more if I make a fool of myself on a regular basis?"

Susan laughed, "I'm saying that people will warm up to you if they see you as open and approachable. Think about it, Hunter... would you trust someone if you didn't know how they were going to react?"

"No, but I wouldn't trust them if I thought they were an incompetent idiot either." Hunter was wondering where the conversation was headed.

"OK, that wasn't a good example. Imagine that you are on your way to work and you get a speeding ticket."

"I take the bus, Susan".

"Hunter, for the sake of my example, humor me. Imagine that you get a speeding ticket. How would you be feeling?"

"Obviously, I'd be in a crabby mood."

"Right, then imagine that one of your employees comes in and tells you about a new marketing campaign that they believe will revolutionize the company and take it in the direction you want to go. Do you listen to them more or less when you're in that bad mood?"

"I don't know... well less, yeah... I'd be less interested." Hunter leaned forward, interested in what Susan had to say.

"That's right, Hunter, even though they had nothing to do with making your mood when you're in a bad mood, you're less likely to trust people. When you're in a great mood, that pushes you to trust more[2]. When you walk into an office you can measure the amount of trust by the ease and camaraderie you see and feel. Crooks like Bernie Madoff[3] used that to his advantage since people talked about what a great guy he was and how he always put people at ease. With people like Madoff, the rules of trust don't apply."

"So how am I supposed to trust anyone then?" Hunter wondered out loud.

Susan was quiet and thought about her response before she answered, "Give yourself a moment and do a check in."

"What do you mean by a check in?" Hunter asked.

---

2 Schweitzer and Dunn – Feeling and Believing: The Influence of Emotion on Trust – University of Pennsylvania

3 Bernie Madoff – Ponzi scheme that embezzled 50 billion from investors

"See if you are tensing up. I know if I'm uptight around someone, my body is telling me something."

"Yeah, I can see that."

"Pay attention to any thoughts that surface," she said with a slight smile.

"Ah, you're saying I have deep thoughts!" said Hunter smiling in return.

"Yes, and I'm saying you have a heart and gut that will give you information too, if you pay attention."

"Whoa ....my heart tells me when I'm workin' out too hard, and my gut tells me when I'm hungry," Hunter said. "What information are you talkin' about?"

Susan smiled and responded. "OK. Here's an example. Think of a time when you were given information to go in a certain direction but you had a strong gut reaction to do the opposite. Would you go with the information or trust your gut?"

Hunter thought before answering. "Well, I didn't follow my gut when I owned my company and I made a mess of things."

Hunter was quiet while he thought over what Susan had said. He looked up and cocked his head to one side and asked, "Have you always been this wise?"

Susan smiled, "I can't take credit for this. I learned about the body, mind and heart scan in a workshop I did out in California with an organization called Six Seconds." [4]

"Weird name for an organization."

---

4 Six Seconds – San Mateo California www.6seconds.org

Susan laughed, "According to Dr. Anabel Jensen, one of the founding members, it takes six seconds for us to change anger to compassion." [5]

"Obviously she's never met my ex-wife," Hunter said with a laugh.

"This kind of self-scan is quick and easy to do – and the best thing is, you can do it anytime and anywhere. It'll help you center yourself and get focused."

"Susan, it sounds like something from the sixties . Do I have to sit cross legged on a cushion and say 'Ommmm'?"

Susan smiled at Hunter, recognizing that many of the things that she took for granted were still not accepted in some business circles.

The body, mind and heart scan was just like it sounded. It was something that Susan did automatically when she was in a situation where she needed to have focus and clarity. Susan would take a moment to scan her body and see if she was tightening or tensing any muscles. She knew from experience that she held tension in her upper back and shoulders when she was stressed, so for her it was a quick reality check on her perceptions of the situation.

Next she would consciously see what thoughts came to mind around the situation. Those thoughts that bubble up to the surface that she didn't always pay attention to. She had learned that she often got great insights from paying attention to those random thoughts.

Finally Susan would take just a second to concentrate on the area around her heart and tune into her feelings, or "heart wisdom." Some people said Susan had incredible intuition, but Susan knew that she'd simply learned to tune into feelings, and that gave her profound insights. The combination of using her whole body to

5 Anabel Jensen – Founding President of Six Seconds and Ei Educator

make decisions was something that she would discuss with others if they asked – but she was also wise enough to know that for some in her company, it was too far outside of their reality to be believed.

"Hunter, this is based on a lot of science." Susan got up from her desk to get a book on her bookshelf.

"Science," Hunter paused and looked at her with eyebrows raised. "Facts. Are we talkin celebrity facts?"

"I'm not getting you. What do you mean? What would celebrity faxes have to do with this?"

Hunter laughed. "Not fax... facts like real information. Not like the weird balding dude who says I have a team of 'people' who checked this out whenever he needs proof that doesn't exist."

"You are such a skeptic!" Susan said before handing him the book. "No, I'm talking real facts. It's based on a lot of science from the Heartmath Institute[6] out of Boulder Creek, California. A Dr. Andrew Armour of Dalhousie University in Halifax, Nova Scotia[7] found a functional heart brain. Here, read the book if you want to know more."

Susan laughed and with a more serious note to her voice said, "It's good to recognize how you are feeling and take that into account when you are making important decisions. When you understand the emotions involved, you have important information that's as important as the cold hard 'facts' in determining what the outcome is going to be."

Susan was known to be someone who had an uncanny ability to read situations and Hunter was starting to see why.

---

6 Heartmath Institute – researchers of Heart Intelligence

7 Dr. J. Andrew Armour discovered a functional heart brain – now with University of Montreal

"OK Susan. Is this that emotional intelligence stuff you're always talking about? I've seen a couple of books and it looks like it's the latest buzz word. New wine in an old bottle." Hunter felt comfortable speaking his mind with Susan.

"Sure, the basic idea of 'emotional intelligence' has been around for a long time... it's a very old bottle indeed. Aristotle talked about it, so did Darwin[8] and most recently Obama's big win in the first election had a lot to do with his emotional intelligence... OK that and social media." Susan laughed "But the new science about emotions blows my mind. Emotional intelligence is an ability. [9]An ability to perceive or recognize emotions in others, but also to figure out your own emotions. I watch you in meetings, Hunter, and you're reading people all the time. I know that you do that well."

Hunter thought about it and said, "Yeah... I'm OK at figuring out how they're feeling but I don't always know how to respond. You seem to know the right thing to say."

Susan smiled. "Thanks. You're right when you say recognizing emotions is only part of using emotional intelligence. You also have to understand how they work, and use feelings effectively, and also to manage emotions in yourself and in other people. People saw a more human side of you today. Leverage that and start talking to people. You know the old saying, 'people do business with people they know, like and trust.' And you took a 'concrete' step that way today." They both laughed. "Seriously through, the way you reacted today shows you're someone people can like. Now show them you like them."

After the meeting Hunter went back to his desk and thought about what Susan had told him. It was a lot to take in and he wasn't completely comfortable talking about his feelings.

8 Charles Darwin wrote "EMOTIONS IN MAN AND ANIMALS" in 1873

9 Dr. Peter Salovey and Dr. Jack Mayer – definition of emotional intelligence as an ability model

His father taught him that you checked your emotions at the door when you walked into work. That if you were the boss, you kept the bad news from your staff and put on a good face so as not to cause panic. That a real man was tough and didn't show emotion.

In the last few months before the business of Birkett Canopy closed down, when he really could have used the support of people around him, he put up a wall and didn't let anyone get close. His anger and sorrow over losing the business were turned inward. That affected how he trusted himself and how he interacted with others. His usual happy-go-lucky personality was hidden by the stress. The only emotion that he felt comfortable showing was anger, and he raged at the world. It alienated all the people who he could have used for support.

Hunter stopped in his tracks with this new thought. Had he really pushed everyone away? What if he was actually responsible for what had happened to him and his company? It was like he was traveling a road he had traveled a hundred times before and suddenly noticed an old landmark. It had always been there but the focus had been elsewhere. With this new insight he saw the past in a totally different way. At that moment, Hunter make a huge decision: he decided to look for a better way to connect with others.

Hunter saw he'd been on a path driven by fear. He was isolating himself because he'd been hurt so badly by his failure at Birkett Canopy. But now we saw another option. He knew he'd stumble a few times but he was determined to make a change.

That very day, Hunter spent the rest of the afternoon getting to know the people he worked with. He started with Matt, the young, fit mechanical engineer who had lent him the too small track suit. After all, Matt and he had shared a lot.

Hunter thought about how Susan treated him. He decided to open his ears, shut his mouth and listen to people. That day, he truly listened for the first time. He asked each of them, "How can I best help you?"

Given the previous few months, at first the team members didn't open up much. They figured all he cared about was the status on their current projects. But in the light of Hunter's new listening, each of them discovered they ended up talking a little more about themselves.

It wasn't strong yet, but that day Hunter made a connection with each of them. They began to see that maybe he wasn't just an "order giver." Maybe he was someone who would actually understand them. It was a good start.

That night Hunter left work at a decent hour. When he walked out the door of Fixtures, the casual "See ya tomorrow" that he got from the team made him feel good. A first glimmer of hope began to lift the despair that had cloaked Hunter since the meltdown.

When he and his wife had decided to call it quits, Hunter walked away with nothing but his clothes and a few pictures. At the time of his divorce, he would have told anyone who listened that he had been screwed and taken to the cleaners but the truth was that he didn't walk, he ran away.

When he rented the apartment, he paid no attention to making it his own place. But that day, when he got home, he looked at his apartment with eyes that saw it for the first time.

It was sparsely furnished with "plain corporate no-style" style. The balcony was the only thing that stood out. He had kept the showpieces from Birkett Canopy and Lounge. He went out to the balcony and felt good. How had his life become so empty? It was like the apartment. Bland beige.

Hunter recalled that one time he'd offered to work with Susan over the weekend to finish a project. She had declined saying, "Work can wait." He was surprised, but she told him that balanced employees actually perform better. Now Hunter could see that he had not been balanced at all for the past year. He had thrown himself into his new job and had neglected his personal relationships and his physical health.

Hunter still had his season hockey tickets, and on a whim he decided to call his daughter and ask her to go with him.

Laura was twelve years old when Hunter and his wife split. Laura'd become very quiet since then. He was so caught up in his own sorrows that it didn't seem to register that Laura was disappearing into her room more and more.

A memory of Laura at four popped into his head and made him smile. He had come home from work and didn't see her until all of a sudden there was a small body in full flight yelling, "Daddy catch me!" He didn't know how he managed to drop everything and catch her. His reprimand to her, "You must let me know before you jump," had no effect. She had said, "But Daddy you'll always catch me." A child's perfect trust. He could feel his eyes mist up.

When Laura was little she used to love sitting beside him while he was watching the hockey game – pestering him with questions, "Why are they mad? Hitting's bad, right Daddy? We like the red ones, right Daddy? Them's have a puck not a ball, right Daddy?" Every question ended with "right Daddy?" as if he had all of the answers to every question.

Hunter picked up the phone and dialed the number that he knew by heart.

"Laura, it's Dad." Hunter was hoping she wanted to talk to him. "Hey, I've got tickets for the hockey game tonight. Wanna' go?"

There was a hesitation before she answered, "Sure. I'll ask Mom if it's OK." Laura hollered so loudly that Hunters ears rang, "Mom! Phone! Pickup!"

Hunter hadn't thought through all of the consequences of his impulsive action to ask Laura to the game.

"Hi Ellen, I was just calling to see if Laura could go to the hockey game with me tonight. It's been awhile since we've had some time together and it's a game she'd love."

"Hunter, this is a school night. What were you thinking? Anyway, it's not your week to be with Laura. You've missed your scheduled visits for the past two months and once the days are past, you can't reclaim them and just pop in anytime you want. Even though she said yes, I'm the one to decide. Why are you doing this? This is just what I've come to expect from you."

He could feel his face get red and a flash of anger washed over him. He was readying his usual response, which would have started a huge fight, but he caught himself and realized something that Susan had taught him. He paused. He thought about how he was feeling, how Ellen was feeling and how he wanted them both to feel[10]. He knew anger wouldn't get Laura to the game. He calmed himself and put a smile into his voice.

"You're right, Ellen. I should have checked with you first. I feel bad that I haven't been spending enough time with Laura lately and I've missed her. I was hoping you could make an exception if I promised to get her home by 9:30. What do you say? I promise I'll return the favor if you have a special thing planned with Laura on one of my days."

---

10 Chuck Wolfe – Emotions roadmap technique

There was a long pause at the other end of the phone and the line went dead. For a moment Hunter couldn't believe she had hung up on him. He waited a few minutes and then with his heart pounding he called back. This time Ellen answered the phone.

"Ellen, don't hang up. You have every right to be pissed off at me. I'm asking you to give me a chance. If I'm going to be a better father to Laura, you have to give me a chance." Hunter tried not to sound desperate. He held his breath waiting for her response.

"You promise that you'll get her home by 9:30?" Ellen sounded tired. "Hunter, I swear if you screw this up, it will be the last time."

"I won't screw it up, Ellen," Hunter said.

The request had caught Ellen off guard. Hunter could hear the tiredness in her voice. "I could use a break. And it would be great not to be the heavy for a change."

Hunter had been so wrapped up with his own life and problems that he had never fully realized how difficult this had been on Ellen. With a quiet voice he said, "Ellen, I promise... and thank you."

When he went to the door to get Laura, he wasn't prepared for what he saw. His sweet pig tailed little girl that he had seen two months before was gone. The mischievous happy child seemed to have disappeared all together and was replaced by a sullen teenager with too much eye shadow and clothes he didn't approve of. He thought of saying something but held back. He didn't want their first outing in months to start out with a fight, so he swallowed his comments.

Ellen and Hunter had a polite conversation and Hunter reiterated his promise to her about getting Laura home by 9:30. It was a civil conversation – one of the first ones since the divorce where they weren't intentionally trying to hurt each other.

He realized how hard it must have been on Laura each time they had a fight, and when he glanced over at her, he could see her relax and thought he saw a hint of a smile.

When he walked down the sidewalk to his car with Laura by his side, he felt a moment of panic, trying to figure out how he was going to behave with this incarnation of a daughter he felt he hardly knew.

Hunter reflected on the successful day of building relationships at the office and thought of what he had learned.

"Just be yourself and talk to her," he thought to himself,

"Hey Laura, any special boy?" Hunter knew it was the wrong thing to say as soon as it came out of his mouth.

Laura gave him a withering look.

Hunter took a deep breath. He remembered Susan telling him to notice people's feelings.

"Laura, I'm sorry I haven't been around much lately. You must feel pretty angry at me," Hunter spoke quietly.

Laura turned and looked at him. He could see hurt, not anger in her eyes. "Yeah, well, I guess yer busy."

Hunter was prepared for anger. The hurt cut him more. This wasn't something he could fix with one night out. This wasn't how he wanted her to feel.

"I've screwed up, kid. But I know I can do better. How about if we have a dad and daughter date every week? We'll take turns picking what to do. Tonight I picked hockey. Next week it's your pick," Hunter spoke quietly with conviction.

"Sure, whatever." Laura kept her head turned towards the window. As usual, his first impulse was anger. He was trying here! But he also felt guilty when he looked at her, knowing that he had spent a year when he was unavailable to her or anyone. "Suck it up, Hunter," he thought. "Feeling guilty isn't going to get you where you want to go."

He wanted Laura to feel excited and happy when they were together. He also knew that he wanted her to trust him again.

As a senior executive in charge of marketing, he was used to putting together plans to get and keep business. He knew a lot about getting clients on board. With clients, he knew it wasn't the first rejection that mattered – you gotta keep at it. Could he do that with his family?

Deep down he believed that Laura wanted to have a great relationship with him just as much as he wanted to have one with her. That hope and belief fueled Hunter and gave him the push he needed to keep engaging her in conversations and asking her questions even when her reply was more of a grunt then a word. Her practiced indifference cracked when the action on the ice heated up. When a goal was scored in the last minute of the third period of the game, giving their team the winning goal, Laura jumped up and down and threw her arms around Hunter's neck.

For the rest of the evening she chatted away, letting him peek into her world with snippets from her life and stories of her friends. Some of what she said bothered him. But the guard was coming down and Hunter knew that his actions could make her put it up again in a heartbeat, so he was very very careful not to react.

When Hunter dropped Laura off, the clock registered 9:28. Ellen was standing at the window and he could see her smile when the car drove up. Laura surprised Hunter by turning and giving him a kiss on the cheek before jumping out of the car. He knew then that they would be OK.

On the drive home, Hunter thought to himself that in the memories of great days, this day would be in the top ten.

CHAPTER 3

THE BALANCED REALITY - RELATIONSHIPS

H unter's office was on the executive floor and had all of the accoutrements of his senior position. The view in his office overlooked Lake Ontario and if he wasn't focused, the boats and the moving landscape distracted him. In order to keep focused, he had his desk moved so his back was towards the window and he faced people as they walked through the door. There was a large sideboard against one wall that held a small mini fridge filled with water and energy drinks. The desk was organized and the docking station that held his computer was the latest in technology. He was known as a techno geek and if anyone wanted to know the latest technology gadget, they knew to ask Hunter. But that was it; like his apartment, he hadn't really moved in. When Hunter looked at his office, he realized that it didn't let people know much about him.

There was a framed poster on the wall with the Fixtures Values, left by whoever had this office before:

"To those who are competent, who commit, are consistent and above all, care... I trust all."

The words were on a picture showing a team wearing the Fixtures uniform working in a refugee camp in Haiti. He knew that the company regularly supported staff initiatives to help out in countries that had faced disasters and Susan had pictures from her time in New Orleans cleaning up houses that had been devastated during Hurricane Katrina.

When he moved into the office, he had thought that the posters were corny and he was going to take them down, but he changed his opinion when he saw his staff react positively to them. At the time, the words meant next to nothing. But now, he started to wonder what could happen if he paid more attention to this stuff. If he was really honest, deep down those words touched something in him.

He thought about Susan's office and the way she'd arranged things so people could have "real conversations," as she called them. Hunter figured, "can't hurt to try..." and decided he would bring in a couch and a couple of chairs so he could move from behind his desk when he was talking to his staff and start holding his meetings in comfort.

He pulled the picture from his briefcase that had been taken at the game that he'd attended with Laura a couple of weeks ago and set it on his desk. The backdrop for the picture looked like it was at centre ice and the props made it look like he and Laura were facing off. The picture showed a middle aged man with a slight paunch and a young girl with too much blue eye shadow and blue nail polish wearing tight jeans. Hunter saw so much more than the image that was captured in the photo. He saw his daughter laughing and enjoying herself. It just felt great to know it still might be possible to get their relationships back on track.

By 11:00 a.m. he realized that he had been so engrossed in getting his paperwork done that he had missed the staff meeting at 10:00. Forgetting the meeting was definitely a mistake. He sent a quick email to his staff and made a note to sit down with each of his managers. In the meantime, he needed the update so he jotted a quick email:

The little pang of guilt he felt at missing the meeting was swallowed up by the huge pile in his inbox. The morning rushed by as Hunter raced to get the last of the paperwork for month end done and completed to send to Susan. When it was half done, he stopped, took off his reading glasses, and swung his chair around to drink in the view. The beauty of the landscape seemed never ending and he took a moment to appreciate it. He had been at the office since 7:30 p.m. and it was the first moment he had paused. He swung back to his desk. It was 1 p.m. and his stomach growled. It reminded him of the 1:30 reservation he had made at Umberto's Bistro.

To: Marketing Team
c.c: Susan.cannon@fixtures.com
Subject: Update from this morning's meeting
Sorry - missed the meeting this morning.
Stanley - please advise me of your team's progress on the new faucets being custom designed for Hope Hospital. What is the delay all about?
Michelle - did you receive all of the information that you needed?
Christine – I've seen the latest reports from your department. Looks great. Go ahead with initiative. Call me with final numbers.
   Please respond by end of business day.
   ~ H ~
Hunter Birkett DBA, B.A.
   V.P. Marketing – Fixtures North American Division
   Hunter.birkett@fixtures.com
   1-905-555-3313

He saw that twenty five new emails had come in since he had sent his message to the team an hour before and decided that he would read them on his BlackBerry while he was at lunch.

When he walked out he called out to Louise, his executive assistant, "I'll be gone for a couple of hours, Louise. If someone needs to reach me, they can call me on my cell."

"OK Mr. Birkett. By the way, Stanley Kowolski came by this morning. I told him you were busy. He wants to set up an appointment with you." Louise was working on her master's degree part time and Hunter knew she was over qualified for the job of executive assistant. When he talked to her about his concerns of her over qualifications, she said that she liked being able to leave the job at the end of the day and be able to fully focus on her studies. A more complex job would be more demanding and working as his assistant gave her the proper balance.

"Did he say what he wanted?"

"No. He did seem upset about something though." Louise was adept at reading people and Hunter felt lucky to have her and Susan fill in the blanks when he was having trouble figuring out what people were feeling.

"Ok. Thanks Louise." Hunter felt himself getting worried. He wondered if it was his imagination. But every time Stanley's name was mentioned he got a little jolt of discomfort. He hurried to the elevator so he could get out before someone saw him leave.

It had been a few months since Hunter had gone to his favorite restaurant in the Beaches area. The Bistro was set back from the road and had an outdoor and an indoor patio that made you feel you were in Tuscany. Hunter loved the laid back ambiance. It was close to his old office and had been the place that he went whenever he wanted to really connect with a customer. The food was always fresh and it was the only place Hunter had found that served his favorite Italian dish. It wasn't a regular menu item, but Hunter had gotten a text from the owner letting him know that it was on the menu today and his mouth had started watering at the thought of it. The 30-minute drive was worth it.

"Ciao, Mister Hunter. Benvenuto! Buono per vederla," the owner exclaimed with a gesture indicating that Hunter should follow he said, "Venite, venite!"

"Ciao, Umberto. It's good to see you too." Hunter walked with Umberto, knowing he would be sat at his favorite table.

Hunter didn't know much Italian beyond how to order lunch, but the warmth and genuine greeting needed no translation.

When he sat down, he smiled and said, "Umberto, I'm hoping you still have what I came for."

"Si. Mister Hunter, I would not sell the last one knowing that you were coming. I will bring you best Osso Bucco outside of Trieste. Deliziosa. You want some bread and oil while you wait?" Umberto didn't wait for Hunter to reply and walked off to start the parade of dishes that would be Hunter's lunch.

Umberto had been in Toronto for over twenty years. He'd followed Jan, a Canadian girl whom he had met when she was backpacking through Europe. They had fallen in love and she convinced him to move to Canada where they married.

Jan was an accomplished artist and her art was bought and sold around the world. Her paintings were on the walls of Umberto's restaurant and added additional charm and sophistication. Umberto had a Master's degree in Philosophy from the University of Milan but had been unable to find work in his field and, like many talented people, went to work in a restaurant while he was searching for employment in his field.

He had started working in the kitchen at the Bistro when it was a local pub and introduced some of his favorite dishes into the menu. He discovered that he loved the restaurant business and had a natural talent as a chef. Within five years he owned it and the pub became "Umberto's Bistro", one of the top Italian restaurants in the city.

While Hunter was waiting, he pulled out his phone and started going through the messages. He didn't feel guilty about being out of the office since he regularly put in ten to twelve instead hour days and Susan had been bugging him to get more balance in his life.

Many of the messages he skipped through, knowing that they could wait until he returned to the office. The message from Stanley read:

> To: hunter.birkett@fixtures.com
> c.c: Susan.cannon@fixtures.com
>
> Subject: re:Update from this morning's meeting
>   Progressing as expected. Updated all at meeting. What delay are you talking about?
>
>   Regards,
>
> *Stanley*
> *Stanley Kowalski, P.Eng.*
> Dir. Product Marketing – Fixtures North American Division
> stanley.kowalski@fixtures.com
> 1-905-555-3313

"Shit!" Hunter muttered. Annoyed, Hunter typed off a quick reply to Stanley telling him that since he was not in the meeting that he had not been updated and that according to the timelines that had been established, the product was two weeks behind schedule.

"That must be one heck of an interesting email," a feminine voice broke his concentration and made him look up.

Hunter looked at the person who was talking and was surprised that he hadn't noticed the attractive redhead when he walked in. She was sitting by herself at a table. In her hands was a book that she had been reading a few moments before. The book was a Henning Mankell[11] mystery; Hunter recognized the title.

---

11 Swedish author Henning Mankell – Books feature crime fighter Wallander

"Ah, I see you like Swedish mysteries. Have you read the Steig Larsson[12] books?

"Yes. I enjoyed the first two more than the last one. Interesting author."

They chatted for a few moments before Hunter stood up and introduced himself.

"Hi, I'm Hunter Birkett. How did you discover my favorite restaurant?"

"Hi, I'm Adrianna Juliet Cosimo, but my friends call me A.J.. Umberto is my cousin."

They chatted for a few minutes about food and Italy and the easy banter between them would have made people think that they had known each other longer than a few moments.

So engrossed were they in the conversation that they weren't aware that Umberto had been watching them from the kitchen.

He came and stood between the two tables and said, "Please, we are getting busy and will need more table. Instead of yelling across room, I move one to the other."

Hunter looked around and could see that the place wasn't that busy, but he was happy to oblige. For the next hour, A.J. and Hunter laughed and talked like old friends. The food was brought out and Hunter couldn't remember when he had tasted anything better. It was well past 3:00 p.m. when Hunter finally realized the time and had to leave.

"I'd love to continue the conversation another time. Would it be OK to call you sometime?"

---

12 Swedish author Steig Larsson – 1954 – 2004 – Trilogy – Lisbeth Salander

It felt so natural to ask that for a moment Hunter forgot that this was someone he had just met and he was asking her out on a date.

A.J. smiled and reached in her wallet. She pulled out a business card that read A.J. Cosimo – Teacher – Special Needs. It had all of her contact information.

Before Hunter could stop himself he said, "You're a special needs teacher? I bet you get a lot of comments on that!"

As soon as the witticism came out of his mouth, Hunter wanted to sink in a hole. He could feel his face flush.

"I'm sorry. I really don't know why I said that."

A.J. looked at him and laughed pleasantly, "Don't worry, I've heard it before."

Hunter laughed and smiled at her appreciatively. He thought to himself, "I can imagine she's heard it a few times."

He awkwardly extended his hand. "I look forward to seeing you again."

When he walked out the door Umberto was beaming at him.

"My cousin... she's beautiful. Si?"

"Si, Umberto, Si."

FIRES BACK AT THE OFFICE

Louise was waiting for Hunter and the look on her face told a story he didn't want to read.

"What's up?"

"Let's talk in your office. There are a few things that I heard while you were out that you should know about."

"This doesn't sound good."

He opened the door and they walked through.

"Hunter, missing this morning's meeting caused more of a stir then you'd think. I overheard Stanley talking and he sounded pissed. Something about you not caring about the company or the staff as long as you make your numbers."

"Seriously? It wasn't a strategic meeting... just an update. All of that can be done by email... in fact I sent one around to all the managers asking for the information. I don't need to see their faces in order to manage them. And as for the rest of that..." He was annoyed that missing the meeting had been blown out of proportion.

"Louise," Hunter said, "Call all of the managers and ask them to meet me in my office. It looks like I need to do some damage control and rein this in before it gets out of hand."

Louise smiled. "I'll do that right now."

"Wait... let me change that. Reserve the large board room and invite the whole team. I heard Jean-Marc is in town right now so we have everyone. Make it for 4:30. I have a few things to do first. "

Hunter knew it would give him time to talk to Susan before the meeting and find out what she had heard.

Susan's office wasn't that far from his. Her door was open so he walked in and shut it behind him.

"Susan, I need twenty minutes of your time. It looks like I've got to do some damage control."

"Really? What's up?"

"I missed this morning's meeting. It wasn't an important meeting and from what I heard some of them are making a big deal about it."

"So how are you thinking of handling it?"

"I'd like to tell them to get over it!"

"OK, Let's play that out. You missed a meeting and now you're going to tell them to get over it. How is that going to go down? Did you apologize?"

"Yah, I sent an email."

"I read that email – maybe it's not a big deal, but do you really think anyone reading it would get a feeling that you were actually sorry?"

"But it's just an update..."

"Look Hunter, if you want my help, let's get real about this. You know that you did something wrong or you wouldn't be here. Missing the meeting sent a big 'I don't care that much' message, and your email didn't make it better. I don't mind that you screwed up, but it's time to man up and fix it. Right?"

Hunter was not used to this kind of directness from Susan, but he knew she was one hundred percent right. While the meeting wasn't a big deal in itself, he broke a promise to his people. "Ok. Tell me how to fix it." His direct, open answer was all Susan needed.

"In order for an apology to be effective you need to bring in the five R's.[13] You first need to recognize the offense. I'm thinking that

---

13 Effective Apology: Mending Fences, Building Bridges and Restoring Trust by John Kador

it wasn't the meeting but what the meeting represented to the team about your commitment to them. The second R is around responsibility. No excuses. Take responsibility for your mistake."

"I get it – I'm not going to pretend it was no big deal."

"Good, then you can go to the third R, which is remorse. When you say 'sorry' you've got to mean it. If you don't, you may as well not bother. An insincere apology is just a brush-off. The fourth R is restitution. This is one of the most important of the R's because it shows you are serious about putting some concrete actions into effect and showing sorry rather than just saying it. Tell them and show them what you are going to do."

"OK – so, I admit and own up. Real apology. Then maybe I can commit to something like a one to one meeting with each of them this week."

"Try that – and go to their offices for the meeting so they know you're the one making the effort. Then the last R," Susan said, "is repetition. It's something that will show them that you are serious about not repeating the behavior. It's taking restitution forward."

"This seems like a lot of apology for missing one small meeting. I'm willing to talk this over to my staff but I don't want to appear weak."

"Hunter, the strength of a leader is measured in the amount of trust others have placed in them. You need to ask yourself whether this will strengthen or diminish your trust quotient. Trust yourself first. If it doesn't feel right, then don't do it. Others will sense your insincerity if you give an apology because I've told you to. I'll respect your decision to do the right thing."

Hunter left Susan's office in deep thought. The meal he had enjoyed earlier in the day was now giving him heartburn and he could feel the start of a headache. He thought of ignoring the whole thing.

He knew he wanted his staff to trust him like he trusted Susan. Over the last month, he'd noticed that people were opening up more, his efforts were working. Communication was easier and productivity had increased. He didn't want it to slip.

Before the meeting Hunter went into his office and wrote down the names of the people he worked with. Then he thought about the level of trust with each person.

Susan Cannon had his unconditional trust and he knew that she trusted him as well. His assistant Louise was put in the same category.

Michelle Ceder, in charge of marketing, was reserved and Hunter knew that he could trust her work abilities. He wasn't sure about whether or not he would trust her to defend him if others spoke badly of him but thought she might.

One by one Hunter went through the list of those who worked for him. It wasn't long before he noticed something surprising. There were a few people who he though something like, "She doesn't fully trust me." Those same people where the ones Hunter didn't fully trust. Trust was reciprocal. He trusted others to the same degree that they trusted him. They trusted him in accordance with how much he trusted them. With that realization, he was ready to start his meeting.

Hunter stood at the door of the boardroom and greeted everyone as they came in. The meeting had already started when Stanley arrived five minutes late and wearing a scowl.

"Hi Stan. You haven't missed much. I was going over the agenda for the meeting," Hunter said.

"Strange time for a meeting. Is this about this morning's email that you sent?" Stanley asked in a way that telegraphed his displeasure.

Hunter turned, smiled and nodded at Stanley and then addressed the group.

"In a way it is about this morning's meeting. I'd like to apologize for missing it. I've said that communication and trust are important in this team and I meant it. I didn't demonstrate those values and I can promise you it won't happen again."

He looked around and could see the words were having the affect he had hoped for.

"We've been working together for a year now and I know and truly believe we need to trust each other in order for us to succeed."

He paused for effect before he went on.

"I will continue to take on any advice or information on that basis and you can count on me to back you and support you a hundred percent. To make up for missing the meeting this morning, I'd like to come see each of you this week to get your updates – so today and tomorrow I'll drop by.

Now as for the matter of meetings... I have asked Louise to schedule a meeting in this boardroom every Wednesday at 9:00 a.m. Louise has been told that I will not take any other appointments at that time and she'll keep that time free for me."

Jean-Marc looked concerned.

"Hunter, I'm sometimes not here on Wednesday. Will you expect me to drive in from Quebec each Tuesday night for a one-hour meeting? Je ne peux pas. Impossible." Jean-Marc looked worried.

"Jean-Marc brings up a good point. There will be times when your schedule doesn't allow you to attend. If you can call in, I'm hoping that you will. This is my commitment to you. I trust that you will do what is best for you, your clients and the company. If you're not here, I know it's for a good reason. But I'll be here and whoever can make it, I'll be looking forward to listening.

Now I'd like to ask each of you to take a moment and fill the rest of the team in on what's taking up most of your time and how each of us can help."

The rest of the meeting was spent talking about the company's direction and plans in the marketing area. Hunter informed each of them how their work related to the company's goals and answered questions about what the future plans were for marketing.

When he got back to his office at six, the light on his phone was flashing, indicating that he had a message. It was a call from Susan asking him to come in and update her on the meeting. Although the call came in at five, she was still there when he showed up.

"How'd it go?" she asked.

"Good. I'm glad I talked to them and I've made the commitment to the team that I would hold a meeting every Wednesday."

"Hunter, I'm going to have to take a really short call in a couple of minutes. I hope you don't mind."

Susan usually turned her phone off when someone was in her office, so Hunter knew that this had to be important.

"Not at all. I can leave and come back later," Hunter said.

"Not necessary. It's an assisted living home that I've been trying to get Harry into and they said they'd give me a call back and let me know if a room was available."

They talked for a little while and when the call came in, Hunter relaxed and walked over to the wall of photos on Susan's wall. While he was looking at them, he stuck his hand in his pocket and came across the card that A.J. had given him.

A smile crossed his lips.

He decided to ask her out and sat down and pulled out his phone and looked for the card that had A.J.'s contact information.

He was anxious for Susan to get off the phone so he could ask for her advice on dating. When she got off the phone, he told her about meeting A.J. and said that he was right now in the process of texting her to ask her out and wondered if he should put a smiley icon at the end.

Susan looked aghast.

"Hunter please don't tell me that you are going to text her? Good God man, you've got to know that is not the way to win a woman's heart!"

"Susan, I've been out of the dating game for sixteen years. I don't have a clue what to do."

"OK. Listen up! Communication in business or romance shares some common rules if you want to build relationships. Face to face first. If you can't do that, then phone. If you can't do that, then email. If you can't do that, then text and follow up with a call. Got it?"

Hunter took a deep breath.

"OK. I'm going home now. I'll call her when I get home, after I've had a few minutes to work up the courage. What am I going to say?"

Susan laughed.

"How about starting with 'I'd like to see you again'?"

That night was the start of his romance with the woman who would become the second Mrs. Birkett.

CHAPTER 4

PUTTING IN THE INVESTMENT – THE 5 C'S OF TRUST

Hunter kept his word and never missed another Wednesday meeting. "No matter what's happening, Louise, don't mess with the morning meeting," he told his secretary. Wednesdays were sacrosanct. Everyone in the marketing department showed up for the meeting at 9:00 a.m. promptly. The meeting went until 11:00 a.m. and they reviewed what they had accomplished in the last week and discussed any problems they had. It was a time when they could strategize what still needed to be accomplished and gain expertise from others in the group.

After almost losing the trust of the people who had worked for him in his department by not keeping his commitments, he knew that once he had set the expectations, his job was to keep his promises and communicate to his staff so they all understood what was expected. If he made a mistake, he circled back and took ownership of it. He made it clear that there was no hidden agenda.

His staff shared what they were working on and both he and his staff honored the decisions made at those meetings.

Gone were the days of Hunter being in the dark. Hunter's openness and commitment to those meetings (and following through every other day) made his department one of the best places to work in the company. Hunter set reasonable goals and communicated what those were to everyone. But it wasn't all a "bed of roses."

One of the biggest challenges was Stanley Kowalski. Just as he had done on that first Wednesday, in the last three meetings, Stanley had arrived late and had disrupted the meeting at inappropriate times. Hunter's attempt to talk it over with him seemed to go nowhere, and his frustration was starting to bubble over.

Hunter didn't want to go back to the "old Hunter" – that guy would have just shut Stan out, shut him down, and pushed him away. It would have "sort of worked," but it would have also undermined trust. He knew that before he started disciplining Stan, he wanted to talk to Susan.

Hunter knocked on the door of Susan's office and walked in. Susan was sitting with her head down, typing furiously at her computer. She put up her index finger and said, "Hunter, give me a moment to complete this thought and I'll be right with you."

Hunter would continue to work on his computer when someone came into his office. "I'm multi-tasking. Don't worry. I'm listening," he would say. He missed the annoyed looks he got when his head was down and he was working on his computer. "Say that again. I missed it," was an oft repeated phrase during his meetings.

Susan would stop everything and focus completely on the person. It was one of the things that Hunter really appreciated about her, and he failed to see the irony in what he appreciated in others and how he acted. The two were often at odds with each other.

Susan had divided her office into three work zones. She had a workstation, which was her desk and held her computer and files, her communication station that consisted of a couch, two comfortable chairs and a coffee table, and her electronic white board and fully optimized computer station where she brainstormed. She knew from her studies that people were less, not more, productive when they multitasked and it was a source of frustration with her that Hunter didn't get it.

Hunter stood waiting for a couple of minutes until Susan finally looked up and said, "There, finished. Take a seat. You've got 10 minutes of my undivided time. Will that be enough?"

Hunter shook his head no.

"Susan, I'm having trouble with Stan. I just don't think there's any way we can work together. He doesn't seem to care about the success of his department and now he seems to question my competency." Hunter ran his hand through his hair, clearly agitated.

Susan moved from behind her desk to one of the comfortable chairs and motioned to Hunter to take the seat so they were sitting next to each other. There was no desk to separate them and Hunter always felt more comfortable telling her what was on his mind when they were sitting in the chairs. He wouldn't have been surprised to find out that Susan had set up her office with that intention.

"OK, since we've only got 10 minutes, do you want to start the discussion now or do you want to hold off until we have more time?"

"Let's start it now and then book more time later." Hunter knew that he needed to calm down and he was hoping that this break would give him a bit more perspective.

"Where to start?" Hunter lowered himself into a chair opposite Susan. "Stan questions everything I ask him to do. If I hear him say 'That's not the way we've done it in the past,' I swear I'm going to lose it. He fights me on every detail. The guys' a dinosaur and wouldn't recognize a good idea unless it came from Moses."

Susan nodded in understanding. "I can see that you're frustrated, Hunter. How do you think Stan might be viewing the situation?" Susan queried.

"Seriously, Susan? I'm supposed to see it from his perspective?" Hunter felt even more exasperated. "Shouldn't he be working hard to get his boss, me, to trust him? I just don't remember ever having these problems with staff when I was in my old company."

Susan smiled, "Isn't that one of your complaints about Stan... that he keeps invoking the 'good ol days'?" Susan leaned forward. "Hunter, I know Stan can need more stroking than other employees but he has a lot of great experience and I've always known him to be a workhorse who gets the job done. What have you done to show him you respect him and his contribution to the team?"

The talk wasn't going the way Hunter had expected. He thought he would walk in and have Susan give him the go ahead to get rid of Stan. Instead, she was asking him what he had done to show Stan that he valued and respected him. It wasn't what he wanted to hear.

"Leadership is tough, If you want people to trust you, you have to trust them first." Susan touched Hunter's arm for emphasis.

"What about earning my trust?" Hunter said with resentment, "If I just let everyone do what they want my department would be a mess. You can't really be advocating that I blindly trust everyone on my team."

Susan smiled again, "I'm not telling you to let people do what they want. The company would be a mess. Different people need to be managed at different levels."

She went to her desk and pulled out a sheet. "You have to manage people according to their level of competency. The hardest part is knowing where to assign people. You want to match the level of authority with the competency level. Leadership is determining the level of authority so the person feels empowered and doesn't feel micromanaged." She returned to her seat and sat down. "Hunter, people want to be trusted. They respond positively to it."

"Sounds like manipulation," Hunter growled.

"No." Susan leaned forward again. "It's the most effective way of relating and working with people AND for getting the results you want."

She pulled out her reading glasses that gave her the look of a librarian and read it over before handing it to Hunter. She looked prim peering at him over her glasses as he read it over.

COMPETENCY LEVELS

1. "Wait to be told," or "Do exactly what I say," or "Follow these instructions precisely."
2. "Look into this and tell me the situation. I'll decide."
3. "Look into this and tell me the situation. We'll decide together."

4. "Tell me the situation and what help you need from me in assessing and handling it. Then we'll decide."

5. "Give me your analysis of the situation (reasons, options, pros and cons) and recommendation. I'll let you know whether you can go ahead."

6. "Decide and let me know your decision, and wait for my go-ahead before proceeding."

7. "Decide and let me know your decision, then go ahead unless I say not to."

8. "Decide and take action – let me know what you did (and what happened)."

9. "Decide and take action. You need not check back with me."

10. "Decide where action needs to be taken and manage the situation accordingly. It's your area of responsibility now." [14]

When Hunter finished reading, Susan said, "Hunter, once you've figured out what the level is to manage each person at, you can trust them to do the job. You need to combine the right level of management with trust. As you mentor and develop the person, you can move them down the list; however, some people may never want or have the skills to be at a ten. Where would you put Stan on the list?" Susan glanced at her watch.

"I'd put Stan at a four."

Susan raised her eyebrows. "Hmmm. That may be part of the problem you're having with Stan. I've worked with Stan on many different projects and I was quite comfortable giving him the go ahead – I'd have put him at a seven or eight. It sounds like there is something else going on."

---

14 Bob Brooks 2010

She checked her watch again. "Hunter, I'm scheduling more time for this. I don't expect an answer right now, but I'd like you to give this list some thought and figure out where you would like to put people on your team. Then work out a plan to move your staff further down the list. Let's get together tomorrow... say 1:00 and discuss this further."

Hunter stood to leave, "Okay, and now I'm curious. Where am I on your list?"

Susan smiled, "You tell me."

Hunter looked over the list. "I know I wasn't there a few months ago, but now I'd guess I'm an eight and working up."

"You're a quick study, Hunter... and I'd agree. I'll look forward to talking with you tomorrow."

When Hunter left Susan's office, he recalled Susan's advice about emotions. "Feelings are real, and they drive people — even if you're not noticing them."

Hunter figured that if Susan was right about Stan's competence then he was probably feeling disrespected and micromanaged by all of the questions and confirmations that Hunter was asking of him. If he was honest with himself, he knew that he was checking up on Stan more than he was with the others because he disliked him and he saw a lot of inconsistency in how he acted. He could see that Stan feeling disrespected wasn't helping the project get done and the rest of the team could feel the animosity between them and it seemed to make them less productive.

"What is it about this guy that gets under my skin?" Hunter wondered. He decided to list all of the reasons that Stan bugged him and all of the reasons Stan was a benefit to the team. He also knew that if he couldn't reconcile the way he felt about Stan, then one of them would have to go… and Hunter had decided that he wasn't moving.

He didn't have to love the guy but he did want his team to be a success, so he needed to find a way to work with Stan or move him to a department where he could benefit the company. Hunter wanted to work with people that he could fully support.

Hunter went back to his office still feeling put out and pulled up the report that Stan had sent him on the large Hope Hospital account that they were trying to secure. The Hope Hospital account was one of the biggest contracts he had worked on since joining Fixtures and Hunter was anxious to prove himself by nailing it.

Like a chef planning a menu, Hunter's marketing background taught him to offer a lot of options before laying out the final meal. Stan was in charge of Product Marketing but his background was in engineering and he seemed to look for one "best" answer.

Stan's proposal was extremely detailed, yet somehow it wasn't complete – it was missing the flair that would make this company bite. While Hunter was reading it, he thought, "He's always grilled chicken without any seasoning." He found Stan boring and finicky and realized that those feelings were pushing him to distrust Stan.

Sitting at his desk, Hunter looked at the list of coworkers who reported to him. He decided to figure out where he would put each of them on the Susan's one to ten list.

Hunter had nine people reporting to him.

Stanley Kowalski was Director of Product Marketing and Hunter always had the urge to yell "Stella!" when Stan walked into the room as a nod to the 50's movie "Streetcar Named Desire" starring Marlon

Brando. Somehow, he knew that Stan had heard it before and with his dour personality, he didn't think Stan would find it funny.

Three staff members reported to him, and Hunter thought that they were the real talent in the department. He rated each of them a four – the same rating he gave Stan. Jean-Marc Benoit was a francophone from Quebec City who expertly handled the busy Quebec market. Matt Jenkins, the employe who had lent Hunter the tracksuit was on a contract at Fixtures. He took every opportunity to promote his cause to be hired on a permanent basis. is ability to resolve conflicts was well known. His nickname around the office was "Client Whisperer" for his talent of soothing irate customers. It came about after an incident with a screaming client whom Matt had calmed.

Stephanie Staples was a delightful woman who always seemed to be smiling even when the rest of the team was having meltdowns. Stephanie had a natural talent for evangelizing the products with clients so they were lined up waiting for the next design.

He couldn't get a feel for Stan's management style and he was wary about assessing him higher than a five on the delegation scale, even after his talk with Susan and her reassurances. The person she talked about and what he saw were at odds. From what he could observe, Stan's success had more to do with the abilities of the people he had working for him rather than his own skills.

Michelle Ceder was a brilliant analyst who Hunter put at a ten plus. Michelle seemed to be able to pull rabbits from thin air and Hunter was sure that she knew what the competitors were doing before they did. A triathlete, she had awards and plaques on her walls from the various races she had been in. She was the only direct report who didn't have anyone working under her and she told Hunter she liked it that way. In addition to the Wednesday meetings, he met with Michelle once a week to be updated on any new research and relied on her sharp instincts in the market. He knew that Michelle could have worked at any number of companies, but she liked the freedom that she had at Fixtures and was engaged to a Research Analyst in another division of the company. She had started to work at Fixtures when she graduated from university and had worked her way up to her present position. The thought was she was a lifer at Fixtures.

Christine Gilbert was Director of Marketing Communications and Hunter had never met anyone so committed to their job. He was comfortable giving her a seven on the delegation hierarchy list and all of her team a five. Her team was the most colorful and unorthodox and although they only showed a few discreet rings and tattoos, he was quite sure they wouldn't get through the metal detector at the airport without setting it off. They always seemed on the edge of anarchy.

Hunter finished off the list and put it aside.

The next day, Hunter was pleased Susan had cleared two full hours to work with him the next day. Her team was top in the company, in part from Susan's unwavering commitment to her staff.

"OK Hunter, you've got my undivided attention. What do you want to discuss?"

"I gave a lot of thought to what you and I discussed yesterday. My concern is around Stan's follow-through. We've sat in meetings together where he tells me that he will get a project completed and in to me on a certain date and so far he hasn't delivered on any of his promises. I'd be okay if he said to me he needed extra time but if he sets the time, then I expect him to honor it or at least get back to me with an explanation." Hunter emphasized the last words.

"Have you discussed this with Stan?" Susan asked.

"Yeah, and it seems to fall on deaf ears. Last time I talked to him, he gave me such a blank stare. I wondered if he was even aware that I was talking to him."

Susan was quiet for a moment and said, "I know you've spent time with most of your staff, but what do you know about Stan?"

"He is the only one out of the nine people who work for me that I can't get a read on. When I brought everyone in to my office, he was polite enough, but now that I think about it, he doesn't tell me a lot about himself. I know what I've read in his personnel report. That he has been at Fixtures for five years and prior to that, he was an Engineering Officer with the military. From what I read he got his degree while he was in the military."

"That's right," Susan said. "He was a troop commander serving in Afghanistan and from what I heard, he had a pretty rough time of it."

"So how the hell do you go from the desert to being Director of Product Marketing?" Hunter looked perplexed.

"He has a degree in Mechanical Engineering and when he came to us he started out as a Product Manager. His ability to make good decisions under pressure is a skill he developed in the military. When the opening came up to head the department, he was the natural pick."

"Susan, what I'm seeing isn't consistent with what you are telling me. I can't put my finger on it but something isn't right. Even in the time I've been here, Stan's behavior has changed. If I didn't know better, I'd say the guy is hitting the sauce."

Hunter expected Susan to scoff at the suggestion but instead she became very quiet.

"Hunter, you may be right. If you are OK with it, I'd like to talk to Stan. I've known him for a long time and I think he might listen to me."

"I appreciate the offer but this is something that I need to do on my own if I'm going to get the respect and trust of my team."

"OK – I know you'll sort it out."

Susan and Hunter were silent for a few minutes. Only a half hour had passed since Hunter had walked in, but he knew there was no more that needed to be said about Stan.

Susan changed the subject.

"I've noticed something else I want to bring up. I see you've built up a lot more trust in your department over the last few months. I'm interested in hearing what you think has made the biggest difference?" Susan leaned forward.

Hunter thought for a moment before he responded. His eyes grew brighter and his voice took on more power.

"It's not just one thing. I think it's a combination. I have to say I've learned quite a few things from watching you. First thing is the open communication. I make sure that nothing interferes with our weekly Wednesday meeting. It's not just on Wednesday though. Over the last month, I realize that I actually care about these people, and I think they are feeling that. I know what is happening with them and I make sure that I show them I appreciate the hard work that they are putting in. I can only do that because they keep me informed of what is happening." Hunter paused while he thought of his team.

"It starts with solid communication," he said. "It's a bit of a chicken and egg thing. They won't communicate with me if they don't think I care about them and they won't know I care if I don't communicate with them."

"There's more, Hunter. What else?"

A confused look came over Hunter and he said, "Yeah, I feel there is, I just don't know how to explain it."

"If you did know, what would you say?" Susan asked. She knew that people often had the answer and gentle encouragement was all that was needed to get at the wisdom that lay close to the surface.

"Like I said, it has to have a solid base of communication. I appreciate the extras that they do and I let them know. I also have learned as much as I could about each of my employees, so I know their extra strengths." Hunter thought for a moment and smiled. "You know, I can get impatient so my team makes sure we're not going over the same things again and again."

Hunter stopped to consider something. "Consistency is where Stan falls down. His work is great one day and crap the next. He's not predictable.

"OK, do you think he has the skills and knowledge for the job?"

Hunter answered immediately, "Yeah."

"So he has the competence; what I'm hearing is all around consistency."

"Yeah, I guess I'd have to agree," Hunter acknowledged.

"OK. It looks like a big dose of healthy 'C's. You said it starts with a base of solid communication, right?"

"Right!" said Hunter. "Followed by showing you care, making a commitment to the individual, showing consistency and competence in action." The look on his face changed and for a moment he looked surprised. He stopped and stared at Susan. "Me." The word hung in the air. "I trust myself again. I trust my own judgment. And as I trust myself more, I'm not afraid to trust others. That's what you were talking about the first day in your office. I get it now."

There was silence as the words sunk in.

"Some people never learn this, Hunter. I know you'll figure out what to do with Stan. Trust your gut." Susan stood up signaling the time was up.

Hunter stood up, exhaled slowly and left the room.

CHAPTER 5

ASSETS YOU CAN BUILD ON – VALUES, ETHICS AND MORALS

On Susan's suggestion, Hunter waited until Monday morning to call Stan. Although he hadn't yet scheduled the meeting with Stan, he had blocked out the morning in his calendar and was hopeful that Stan's schedule was free.

Stopping at his favorite Starbucks, he picked up a latte for himself and Susan and headed for the office. The day was overcast and rainy and didn't do anything to help his mood. Talking to Stan about his negative performance wasn't how he wanted to start the week, but he knew that putting it off and hoping it would resolve itself wasn't the answer.

When he got to Susan's office it was exactly 8 a.m. and she had just arrived and was taking off her coat.

"Right on time, Hunter... as usual." Susan smiled and motioned for him to take a seat on the couch.

"Yeah, I've been thinking about what I could say to Stan and I'm not looking forward to the conversation. I don't want it to go south," he said as he handed her the latte.

Susan gave Hunter a look of support and accepted the latte.

"Thanks," she said, raising the cup in salute, "Hunter, if you were the kind of guy who looked forward to these conversations I wouldn't have hired you."

Hunter took a sip of his latte. Leaning forward, he said, "Susan, why did you have me wait until today? I was all ready to talk to him Friday before he went home. Then at least I wouldn't have been going over and over and over what to say to him all weekend long. It would be done and I could have enjoyed my weekend with A.J."

Susan laughed. "Oh, give me a break, Hunter. As if I'd believe that your weekend with A.J. was ruined."

Hunter grinned sheepishly.

"If you told him on Friday, what could he do? He'd be going over and over what you said and have a weekend to sit in a lot of negativity. You could end up with greater problems than what you started with."

"Yeah well, I can't imagine that there will be anything that I can say that will put a good spin on what needs to be done." Hunter's brow was furrowed in deep thought.

"Look, we don't have a lot of time but I want to explain a way of thinking and being that gets positive results. Have you ever heard about appreciative inquiry?"

"No. And if you tell me that I need to write all the things I appreciate about in Stan, I'm walking out. That guy has been a pain in my ass for the last three of the ten months I've worked here. I think I've let it go on longer than I should have. I'm willing to work with him, but he needs to make some serious changes in attitude and effort."

"Haven't you wondered why?"

"I asked him why and he didn't say a thing."

Hunter's voice was sounding less convincing. When he went over in his head all he was told about Stan, it didn't add up with what he had seen. He knew there had to me more to it.

Susan pressed on.

"Hunter, I have adopted appreciative inquiry as a way of viewing life. And before you say it," she held up her hand, "its not more hippy stuff." Susan preempted Hunter's teasing.

"There are a few techniques for you to use that I know will help you with Stan. There is a particular way of asking questions, so you're focusing on what you want and not what you don't want." Susan looked at Hunter kindly before adding, "Do you really want to spend a whole hour telling Stanley what you don't like?"

"Earlier on Friday I did. Now I'm not so sure."

"Go on," Susan said.

"Do you know that in the last month I've had to send back four of his reports to redo? I spent time that I didn't have. The cost of not trusting him is slowing down the department's ability to close deals. I wasted time going through everything he sent me, even stuff that

I had already looked at and approved, looking for mistakes. He's so friggin inconsistent!"

Hunter was on a rant and Susan knew he was telling her all of this because he could vent without it going any further or coming back to haunt him. "Sorry. End of rant. What's your suggestion?" Hunter asked.

"Appreciative inquiry[15] is a particular way of asking questions, Hunter. It builds on what is working."

"Well, at this moment not much is working when it comes to Stan."

Susan got up from her chair and walked over to her desk. The air conditioning kicked in and rustled a few of the papers that were sitting on top of the desk. Susan picked the papers up and placed them in her top drawer, straightened a couple of pictures and then opened the side file. She quickly flipped through and pulled out a folder. She handed Hunter a sheet outlining a four part process.

"Man, are you always this organized?" Hunter asked.

Susan smiled and said, "Pretty much. Look this over and then I'll explain the concept in more detail."

This is the sheet that Hunter saw...

---

15 Developed by David L. Cooperrider of Case Western Reserve University in the early 80's

APPRECIATIVE INQUIRY APPROACH

Discovery – The best of what is
Deal with the emotions and feelings first
Seek first to understand and then to be understood
Gather as much information as you can

Dream – Imagine what the perfect workplace would be like
Figure out what you really want.
What does it feel like?
What does it sound like?
What does it look and sound like to the rest of your team?

Design – Planning and prioritizing the ideal
Use conciliatory gestures:
· Apologizing
· Self-disclosing
· Owning up to your part and taking responsibility
· Conceding

Destiny – the ongoing implementation for sustaining the change
· Don't back out
· Prevent more challenges

Susan sipped her latte as she waited for Hunter to finish reading, then she said, "The basic idea is to focus the relationship with Stan around what works rather than trying to fix what doesn't. Actually, it works for entire corporations. I've just narrowed the focus so you can use it with Stan."

Hunter spent the next half hour peppering Susan with questions. As they talked Susan could see the tension in his face dissipate and his body relax.

Hunter paused searching his memory and then said, "OK is this the same as that feelings intelligence you talked about earlier?"

Susan smiled. "No, but they complement each other. Emotional intelligence is being smarter with feelings. Appreciative inquiry is one way of doing that – it's using what has worked in the past to build a positive future."

Hunter looked at his watch. The time was 9:10 a.m. He knew that Stan arrived at 8:30 a.m. and he wanted to catch him before he got too engrossed in the day. On the walk back to his office he went over what he was going to say and do.

He used Susan's worksheet to map out the meeting with Stan.

Hunter thought about the emotions roadmap and figured that Stan probably felt as untrusting towards him as he felt about Stan. He wanted Stan to feel comfortable talking to him, but too much friendly chatter would sound phony given their past history. He also wanted Stan to feel open and concilitory. He knew that the tone of the meeting would start with the first words he spoke, so he smiled and picked up the phone.

"Stan, I'm working on the projections for our department and I need your help. How's your morning? Can you spare a couple of hours so we can review some figures?"

The stiff military training that kept his emotions and feelings in check had both helped and hindered Stan. He recognized Hunter's authority and it was ingrained in him to follow orders from superiors so with little emotion he replied, "I can be there in twenty minutes."

When Stan showed up precisely twenty minutes later, Hunter greeted him with a smile and motioned for him to take a seat on one of the new sofas.

Stan noticed the new furniture. Whereas before there was a lot of wasted space and nothing but a desk and credenza, now there was a large area of the office that was set up with two large overstuffed leather sofas and comfortable wing backed chairs. In another corner, in front of the bookcase, there was a coffee table and three chairs.

Hunter started the conversation. "Before we start our meeting I'd like to tell you a little about my background. When I came to this company, I had just gone through a bankruptcy and was pretty pissed off at the world. It took me awhile before I could let that go."

For a few moments, there was silence and Hunter looked out the window reliving what had happened two years before. He turned back toward Stan and leaned forward.

"Now, I didn't call you in here to tell you about my sad tale, but I want you to know that I know what pressure looks and feels like and I know how it can affect you. From everyone I've talked to, they tell me you're one of the best Directors and Managers they've had in the Product Department." Hunter paused to let that sink in then continued, "Stan, I've got to tell you, that's not what I've been seeing. So, I'm asking you to trust me and tell me what's going on."

Stan gave Hunter a hard look and with an edge to his voice said, "I do my job the best I can without complaint." He looked like he was ready to say more but closed his mouth and pressed his lips together as if to hold back a retort.

There was a long moment of silence where the two men seemed to size each other up. Hunter was the first to break the silence.

"Your staff is completely loyal, which tells me a lot. They obviously have a good relationship with you, one based on trust. That's exactly the kind of manager I want to be – and right now, I can tell you and I don't have the level of trust we need. I want this department to be a place where we can all support each other, but if we're not real, that's not gonna happen."

Hunter let the words sink in and looked over at Stan. He knew that this wasn't what Stan had expected... it wasn't originally what Hunter had planned to say when he had walked through the door in the morning.

Stan studied Hunter to see if he was sincere. His shoulders slumped. He no longer looked like he was marching off to war but like a man who had just surrendered.

The agenda for the meeting changed and the projections were put aside. The battle that had waged between the two men was over and Stan opened up.

Hunter learned things that no one knew, not even Susan, and it explained Stan's erratic performance. Stan's wife of twenty years had been diagnosed with breast cancer and had been going through aggressive chemotherapy. Stan's upbringing and military training taught him to park his emotions at the door and he believed he could "soldier through."

Hunter and Stan worked together to come up with a plan that would take some of his responsibilities and distribute them to his team and lighten his workload so he could spend more time at home. The company had a generous policy for a spouse or a parent who was suffering from a major illness and Hunter convinced Stan to take advantage of it.

Stan looked at Hunter and said, "I'm a private guy and I'd prefer if you kept this to yourself. I'll tell people when I'm ready."

Hunter nodded.

"There will be a few HR people who need to know to set up the benefits, but I promise that what you discuss with me goes no further."

It didn't happen overnight. Although people could see and sense the difference in their relationship they were surprised the first time Stan walked into a meeting, late, and without a dressing down from Hunter.

Stan tested Hunter's patience on a few occasions. The first month he tried to stick to the old schedule not really believing that Hunter was sincere. He made mistakes and they were corrected with nothing more than a private conversation between the two men.

By the second month, Stan started to go to Hunter and confide in him when he was feeling overwhelmed. When Stan needed to talk, Hunter was there to listen. He became adept at asking Stan, "What are you feeling?" instead of "How are you feeling?"

It allowed Stan to open up more and talking helped him heal. It opened Hunter's mind to healing the relationships that were important in his life.

By the third month Hunter no longer felt the need to check on Stan's work.

Although people in the office eventually found out about Stan's wife, Hunter was true to his word and told no one. He became the support that helped Stan get through the dark months.

When Stan's wife went into remission and was given a clean bill of health, Hunter was there to help him celebrate.

Hunter was learning to find something to appreciate in all of his relationships and the biggest and most astonishing change was in his relationship with his ex wife and daughter.

FRIENDSHIPS

The house that Hunter had lived in with Ellen was at the end of the cul-de-sac in a quiet and well maintained suburb. When Hunter and Ellen were married he was never around to fix up things that needed to be fixed.

After the night out at the hockey game with Laura, and on a whim, he made the offer to do small things around the house, knowing that he'd get to see more of his daughter.

Ellen was suspect at first, but called him in desperation one day when she couldn't find a plumber to come out and fix a problem pipe.

In a few months, he had spent more time fixing up the house than in the four years he had actually lived there. The change in all of their relationships had started the night he took Laura to the hockey game and it kept getting better. He had been dating A. J. for over a year. A.J. had met Laura and Ellen a number of times and he was grateful and amazed that all three women got along.

Ellen was dating someone she liked and it looked serious. Now that they were both happy in other relationships, they wondered how their marriage had lasted as long as it had.

Ellen's comment to Hunter after meeting A.J. was, "You're good together, Hunter. I hope it works out for you."

Hunter's eyes widened in surprise but the smile didn't leave his face for the rest of the day.

One time when he was over doing his handy work, Laura said, "A.J. had a lush grill," which shocked him into silence. He didn't know how to respond, especially when both Ellen and Laura burst out laughing at his discomfort. He had gone home, looked up teen slang on the internet, and found out she was talking about A.J.s beautiful smile.

A few months later on a hot day in August, Hunter skipped out of the office early. Since both of them were on holidays he'd asked if he could come over and talk to them.

Laura was finished with the overdone makeup and was now in either sweats or her basketball uniform. She was the small forward on her basketball team and, although smaller than most of the girls on the team, she was nimble and had the dexterity that more than made up for her size. Her long hair was pulled into a high ponytail and she looked younger than when he had taken her to the hockey game over a year ago.

Hunter knocked and walked in. Laura was sitting at the counter. Hunter was proud of himself because he'd been studying more teen slang on the web:

"Hey sweetie. You need some cheddar to go pez out?" Hunter said as he pulled a twenty from his wallet.

"Dad, it just sounds creepy when old people try to sound cool and talk like teenagers. If you're asking me if I need some money to hang out with my friends then yeah... of course." She reached over, and with a smile, took the money.

Hunter eyes twinkled and he was going to say something else but a look from Laura silenced him.

Ellen walked in the room and smiled at Hunter. Laura and Ellen exchanged a look that Hunter couldn't decipher.

"I've got something that I want to tell you," Hunter hesitated before continuing. "Actually, it's something that I want to ask you... or not really ask but get your opinion."

He stuttered and stammered for a few moments without really saying anything that made sense.

Finally, Laura went up and put her hand on Hunter's shoulder. "Dad, we really like A.J. Are you going to ask her to marry you?"

Hunter looked surprised. "How did you know that's what I was going to say?"

Both Ellen and Laura laughed.

"Hunter, you've never been good at hiding how you feel. I like A.J., but for the life of me I can't see what she sees in you!" The smile on Ellen's face let him know she was teasing.

"Is it weird that I'm asking my ex-wife and daughter to help me plan my proposal?"

Laura leaned against Hunter and said, "Yeah, but good weird."

Hunter pulled out a small box and opened it. "Do you think she will like the ring?"

"Dad, it's not about the ring. If she doesn't like it, she can pick out another one. Although I think this one is sick!"

"Oh no! I thought A.J. would like it. Maybe I'll wait." Hunter looked frazzled.

"Dad, sick means that I think it is awesome." Laura put a reassuring hand on his shoulder.

Hunter looked relieved. He spent a few minutes talking to Ellen and Laura and headed off to the restaurant.

Hunter went to the restaurant first and dropped off the ring. He had given careful instructions to Umberto, who beamed and kissed him on each cheek and made a great show of welcoming him into the family. Hunter reminded him that the proposal had not yet been accepted.

Hunter had called Umberto at the start of the week and arranged for a special meal. He had waited until the day before to ask A.J. to a movie so she wouldn't get suspicious and told her he would pick her up at six thirty. When he arrived at her door, A.J. was in jeans and looked surprised to see Hunter dressed up.

"What's up,? I thought you said we were going to a movie."

"Ah, right, yeah, we are. First, I thought we'd go to Umberto's for supper. Is that okay?"

"Sure. Let me go change. Berto will give me a hard time if he sees me in jeans. He's old school."

When they arrived at the restaurant, Umberto was over the top, hugging A.J. and Hunter.

Hunter tried to telegraph him to tone it down.

The heat of the day hadn't dissipated and the restaurant was packed. The patio was overflowing, so A.J. said they could sit anywhere.

"No, no, no. For you, I have best place." Umberto grinned from ear to ear.

Umberto took them to the back patio to a place in the corner that had been especially set up. The table was set with white linens and candles and the scent of the bougainvillea mingled with the hot summer night.

A.J. raised her eyebrows and looked from Umberto to Hunter. A smile started in her eyes and moved to her lips and she gave Umberto a hug.

The meal was everything that Hunter had wanted and then some. It started with a small antipasto of special olives, marinated anchovies and delicate cherry tomatoes that had been handpicked that afternoon and drizzled with a balsamic vinegar that Umberto kept for special occasions.

After each course, Umberto would beam and pat Hunter on the shoulder.

"What the heck is up with Umberto?" A.J. asked.

The polenta that followed was delicate and perfectly cooked. It was shaped in a heart and was placed on a bed of fresh tomato sauce and roasted red peppers.

Next was the Osso Bucco that Hunter had specially ordered, followed by a platter of perfectly cooked vegetables.

Dessert was fresh strawberries and peaches served with a Balsamic Zabaglione. When the last dish was taken away, Hunter called Umberto over and said, "Berto, I think you've forgotten a dish."

A.J. looked at Hunter and said, "Seriously Hunter, I couldn't possibly eat anything else. Umberto, please don't bring anymore food."

Umberto smiled and said, "Ah but this is perfect for feeding the soul."

When he came back, he had a covered silver tray. He walked over and with a great flourish took the cover off and presented it to Hunter. The tray held a small blue box that was open showing the diamond.

Hunter reached over and took the box off the tray and then he took the ring out of the box. He got down on one knee.

"A.J., this is where we met. From that first moment, I knew that I wanted to spend the rest of my life with you. Will you marry me?"

Umberto who had been standing to one side clapped his hands and shouted, "Yes! Yes!"

A.J. laughed. "I'm sure it's me he's asking Berto, and my answer is also yes."

With a lopsided grin, she added, "So, I guess we're not going to the movies."

People at surrounding tables started clapping, and a chant started at one table and carried forward and pretty soon everyone was yelling, "Kiss. Kiss. Kiss!"

The mood in the restaurant was festive and it felt like a wedding had already taken place. Umberto stood up and made a speech welcoming Hunter into the family and said he would put in a good word with the rest of the large extended Cosimo clan.

A.J. and Hunter went around and thanked people for their good wishes.

Happiness seems to attract more happiness. In the two years since Hunter had left Birkett Canopy, he had never run into his old friend Rick Phillips, although he had been told by Umberto that he came into the restaurant on a regular basis.

Hunter had heard that Rick had gone to work for another manufacturing company. When he felt a hand on his shoulder and a familiar voice say congratulations, he knew immediately who it was.

He spun around and looked at Rick. He felt a wave of emotions pass over him, surprise, guilt, shame and gratitude and he wasn't sure which emotion was stronger. For a moment, he didn't know what to say.

Sometimes what we need isn't always what we want. In the difficulties of the last couple of years, Hunter matured. He learned lessons from his struggles he would never have learned if his life had been easy. He wasn't the same man that Rick had known in the last year at Birkett Canopy. He was wiser and appreciated his life in a way he never had before.

Over the year, he'd started to pick up the phone to call and talk to Rick many times, but he always stopped himself. He wasn't sure that Rick would talk to him... and he was ashamed of the way he had behaved in his last year at Birkett Canopy. So seeing Rick in the restaurant could easily have pushed Hunter's buttons and made him shut down, but that was the old Hunter. He was ready to be done with shame and blame.

"Rick. It's great to see you." Hunter looked at his old friend and smiled.

"A.J., I'd like you to meet Rick Phillips."

A.J. looked at Rick and tilted her head to one side. She smiled and stuck out her hand. "So, you're the great Rick Phillips. I've heard lots of stories about the trouble you and Hunter used to get into. It's great to finally meet you."

"Wait, let me get my wife. I'm sure she'd love to meet you." Rick left and went over to his table.

They could see Rick's wife glance over at Hunter and shake her head. Rick scowled and said something to her and then motioned A.J. and Hunter over to the table. They could see his wife Anna give him a look that told them he would be paying for that decision later in the evening.

When they went over to meet Anna it felt like the temperature of the room dropped ten degrees. Anna's smile was tight and didn't go to her eyes.

"Congratulations. How lovely that you've found someone new."

Rick shot her a disapproving look.

A.J. went over to Anna and extended her hand. She said, "Hi Anna, I'm A.J. I'm so glad I met you tonight of all nights. I know what you and Rick mean to Hunter."

Anna looked surprised.

"He did tell me that he was a pretty big jerk back when he ran his own company," A.J. turned and smiled at Hunter.

Anna laughed and invited A.J. to sit down.

Rick leaned over to Hunter and whispered, "Man I don't know what you did to deserve her."

Hunter smiled and said, "I don't know either, Rick. But I promise I'm going to be the man that does."

CLARIFYING VALUES

Hunter walked in the next morning and shared his news with a few people he felt close to. By mid morning, as Hunter walked down the hallway, people stopped and offered their congratulations. The grin on his face said it all. Before he knew it, the day was done and he hadn't had a chance to drop in and talk to Susan despite wanting to tell her in person.

At five, he just couldn't concentrate and decided to call it a day. On a whim, he stopped by her office.

"Susan, you got a minute?" Hunter still had the goofy grin on his face.

Susan got up from her desk, walked over to Hunter, and gave him a hug.

"Congratulations, Hunter. I've heard the good news. When's the big day?"

"This is a second marriage for both of us, so we're thinking we'll go to Hawaii and get married on the beach, just the two of us. I wanted to see if it's okay for me to take off for a couple of weeks in November?"

Susan checked her calendar and looked at the dates. When she looked up she was smiling and said, "Well, it's our slow time and I don't see a problem... especially since you still have days left over from last year."

"Great! I'll call and let A.J. know. I've got something else I want to talk to you about as well. Have you got a minute?"

"Sure, what's up?" Susan stood up and moved to her couch.

Hunter followed and sat down. With a more serious tone he said, "Susan, I've made some pretty stupid mistakes in my life and it took me a long time to realize that there was a cost, not just to me but to others I care about. I don't want to blow this. I want to be the guy that A.J. and Laura can be proud of."

"I don't think you have anything to worry about. From what I can see you live your life and make decisions according to strong values."

"Yeah, well I thought I was doing that before and look how I screwed up."

Susan smiled and said, "Do you remember one of the exercises I had you and the other managers do when we were trying to get our teams to embrace the vision and mission of Fixtures? It was called 'Noble Goals[16]' Get those notes out. You wrote some great stuff. If you follow what you wrote, I promise you that it will be a compass that will guide you. What did you put down as your top values?"

Hunter remembered that session. As so often happened when Susan started on the "soft stuff," he'd been resistant at first. But her questions got to all of them that day. She'd asked questions like, "What do you want to be known for after you leave here?" and, "What's the one value you wish everyone would follow?" The discussion got them all fired up about purpose, and purpose is incredibly motivating, but in truth, he hadn't paid enough attention back then.

Hunter closed his eyes for a moment trying to remember, "OK. Well, I know the values are family, trust, community and honesty."

Susan smiled and cocked her head to one side. "Hmmm, I'm curious. Why did you pick them?"

"Well, I love my daughter and I love A.J. They are my family. I'd do anything for them." Hunter looked uncomfortable.

---

16 Noble goals is one of the measured competencies in the SEI – Six Seconds Emotional Intelligence Assessment (www.6seconds.org/tools)

"Relax, Hunter. This isn't a test. It's a process I used to help me figure out what my values are and I thought it might help you clarify things."

Susan leaned forward for emphasis and said, "The key point to remember is that a value energizes everything involved with it."

"And the Noble goals Susan? What's that all about? Why not just 'goals'?"

"We'll get to that in a minute. Let's talk about values first. For me it's only a value if I use it to make the difficult decisions. If you had to pick two, which ones would they be?"

Hunter said, "What kind of man would I be if I didn't say family?"

"For the moment let's take that off the deck. Pick two others."

Hunter considered them carefully before he spoke. "I'd have to say trust and openness. I lost trust in myself and for a while, I was closed off to everyone. When I wasn't operating with those core values, I was of no use to my family, and I wasn't honest with anyone."

Susan nodded. "So often we think we take action because we are motivated to do so. When we peel it back to the centre of our beings, what motivates us is our values."

"But Susan, when I moved to this company I was motivated by the will to survive. I had alimony payments that I had to take care of. I didn't see any values in action... besides a monetary value."

"Seriously? If I remember, you had just gone through bankruptcy. You could have skipped out on your responsibilities, taken a nothing job and never paid alimony."

"Come on, Susan. That was never an option. How could I have looked at myself in the mirror?"

"Hunter, your values were at work when you made those decisions. Let me ask you, why did you pick Fixtures?"

"Because I... OK... I get it. It was because of the reputation as a company that could be trusted, values that the company adheres to."

"Everything I've read tells me that trust is absolutely vital for a company to be ethical.[17] If Fixtures didn't value Trust, I know I wouldn't be here. The fact is, I believe in the company's values and that is the reason I came to work here," Susan said with passion.

Hunter nodded. "And what I've learned is that the more I've trusted and expressed my confidence in others, the more I've been rewarded with their trust."

"That's right. Trustfulness is expressing a sense of confidence in others and trustworthiness is the result of acting in such a way that you gain the confidence of others. Can you see how they are related?"

"Sure. Trust and Trustworthiness have to go together. So we've got my values. Now tell me again about the 'noble goals' thing? Sounds like more of your hippy stuff." Hunter smiled.

Susan laughed. "Your Noble Goal is a statement of purpose that puts all your other goals together. You want to show up for your kid, but why? You want to be a good manager, why? When you have that 'why' clear, it gives you energy and focus. Then, your Noble Goal acts like a compass to help you line up what you are doing, how you are doing it and why you are doing it. Are your intentions coming through in your actions and behaviors?"

---

17 Founded in 1990, the Institute for Global Ethics (IGE) is an independent, non-sectarian, nonpartisan, 501(c)(3) nonprofit organization dedicated to promoting ethical action in a global context.

Hunter looked thoughtful.

Susan added, "In other words, ask yourself the big questions about what you're doing each and every moment. How are you living your life? Are you putting your purpose into action? Your Noble Goal is a reminder—when you're screwing up and going in the wrong direction, you can just ask yourself: 'Am I pursuing my noble goal?' If not, straighten up."

Hunter said, "Yeah, simple stuff. Like the meaning of life and why are we here. So Susan, what is your noble goal?"

Susan smiled. "My noble goal is to encourage integrity. Every day when I've got a tough decision, I ask myself: Will this choice encourage integrity? It actually makes life a lot easier when you know where you want to go."

Susan smiled and looked at her gold watch. Her cream linen suit still looked fresh in spite of the heat and the long workday.

"Speaking of which — it's six and I've promised Harry we'd go out for supper, and if I'm going to follow that Noble Goal I better get a move on. But if you have any questions, let me know and we'll arrange a time to talk tomorrow. After you've had some time to think about it, I'd love to know what your noble goal is."

Just before leaving, Susan turned back to Hunter with a smile, "By the way, we would never have been able to have this conversation when you first came to Fixtures. You've come a long way, Hunter."

CHAPTER 6

INVESTING NOW FOR FUTURE RETURNS – BUILDING TRUST

H unter gave up his apartment and moved into A.J.'s condominium, which had the warmth and charm that Hunter's lacked. "It's my Italian chaos styling," A.J. laughingly said. The overall feeling was one of welcome and refuge from their busy lives.

Since the condo was forty minutes from work and wasn't on a bus route, Hunter justified buying a car. A.J. referred to it as his 'mid life crisis car'. It was a brand new BMW roadster fully loaded and had a retractable hard top. Driving this baby to the office, he listened to loud music and de-cluttered his mind. He relished in the sound and feel of power he held behind the wheel.

"You meditate, I drive," Hunter had said to A.J. when she asked him how he dealt with the pressures of the job.

Today as Hunter drove to the office, his mind shifted to autopilot and he thought of the last five months.

Marriage agreed with both of them. Hunter looked and felt better than he had in years. When he looked at the solid gold band, he smiled at the memory of the ceremony on the beach in Kauai.

A.J. had worn a simple white dress and he was casually dressed in a short-sleeved shirt and khakis. Their only adornment was the fragrant double orchid lei that A.J. wore and the maile style ti leaf lei that she convinced Hunter to wear. She had left her long red hair loose, it cascaded over her shoulders, and the curled tendrils danced in the wind and caught in the petals of the orchid lei.

Hunter found it hard to breathe remembering the moment he looked into her blue eyes and knew they would be together forever.

Both of them were barefoot and only the officiate and the photographer were there to witness the ceremony that took place at sunrise. Hunter had paid extra to have them get them to the beach at 6:30 a.m. so they could be there as the sun rose at 6:46. The only music was the gentle sound of the surf lapping against the shore and the island birds calling to each other.

Hunter and A.J. had huge first weddings that had cost their families as much as a sizeable down payment on a house. They both agreed that the first wedding had been for their families and this one was solely for them.

Rick Phillips had been Hunter's best man at his first wedding and at one point had tried to talk him out of marrying Ellen.

He recalled the conversation at his bachelor party and his brows knit together trying to remember all that had happened. It had not been a sober exchange. Hunter suspected that Rick had been thinking on it for quite awhile, and the liquid courage finally gave him his voice. Vague memories of Rick saying things like, "Ya have nothin' in common, she's highballs and you're paint balls... and she busts your ass all the time man... 'yer never gonna make her happy." They had never talked about it again, but Hunter knew Rick had doubted the match, and in retrospect, Rick had been right.

Hunter and Rick had started talking regularly after their chance meeting at Umberto's on the night of the engagement.

More recently, after the four of them had dinner together, Rick smiled at Hunter and said, "You got it right this time."

Hunter felt that he was on the way to rebuilding the trust with Rick that was damaged when Birkett Canopy went bankrupt. He wanted to be done rebuilding already, and back to the great friendship they'd had. As he merged into the city traffic, he thought about what he had learned in the four years of working with Susan Cannon.

"What was it Susan told me?" Hunter asked himself out loud. "Oh yeah, trust can't be rushed. Real trust can't be manipulated, faked or spun." Although when Susan said it, she was talking about the meltdown in the financial market, Hunter thought it could be applied to almost all of life.

He knew that if he were to rebuild the trust with Rick, he would have to make investments into the relationship through time, commitment, and honest friendship.

The forty minute drive flew by and when he pulled into his underground parking garage, it started to rain. Hunter was glad that he had beat the deluge.

Some things hadn't changed after his marriage to A.J. He was still an early riser and it was only 7:30 in the morning when he arrived at his desk.

He glanced at one of the pictures on his desk. It was taken in Kauai as the sun was rising and as the words, "I now pronounce you..." were being spoken. The look he gave A.J. said everything that he had trouble saying and spoke of his love and happiness with his new bride. He smiled at the memory.

A. J. had been unable to convince Hunter to sleep in and start his day later. "I like getting there before my staff comes in," Hunter told her. "I can clear off some paperwork before the craziness of the day starts pulling me in so many different directions."

His appointment calendar showed that he had a 10:00 meeting with Mark Remacle, the Chief Marketing Officer of Fixtures. Susan was away on holidays for a couple of weeks and in her absence, Hunter was in charge. He was surprised that Mark had chosen this time to meet. He rarely came to their offices and he had never asked to meet with Hunter before.

Hunter knew that winning the Hope Hospital contract hadn't gone unnoticed and that success had opened the door to new opportunities. Hunter's bonus and the bonus for each of his team members eased the pain of the long days and weekends they had sacrificed to win the business. Hunter had made the promise to his staff, and kept it, that the eighty hour week would not be the norm. He expected and wanted a balanced life for all of them.

Hunter noted that the call to set up the appointment came in the day after Susan had left to go on her cruise, when he had no way of contacting her or letting her know.

"Knowing what I've heard of Mark Remacle, it's no accident," Hunter thought to himself.

"Perhaps," Hunter thought, "he wants to see if they can duplicate our success in the Hope account to the rest of the company." Hunter doubted it was that straightforward and his gut told him to be wary.

Mark Remacle was a man with an ego. In a company that had "trust" as its core value, Mark operated outside of the boundaries and danced on the edge – being brilliant enough to know when he was close to the precipice.

If power is the fuel of accomplishment, Mark was high octane, intent on personalizing his power for his own gain. He had taken the company to new heights bringing in incremental revenue, growth, and profitability and exceeded all the targets the company had set for him. He was brilliant and ruthless, and only cared about others according to how much power or influence they could bring to him.

Hunter had met both John Pitt, the CEO and Alessandro Bonvicini, the Chairman of Fixtures and knew them to be men who lived and breathed the company values. He wondered how they kept promoting Mark when he clearly didn't line up with their values . Hunter believed it was because Mark surrounded himself with good people who had the social skills and values that he lacked.

Hunter had once asked someone close to Mark if they really trusted the guy, and the reply was telling.

"I trust Mark to always be Mark," was the reply.

Hunter's phone rang.

It was Bonnie Tilford, Mr. Remacle's Executive Assistant. She got straight to the point,"Mr. Remacle will see you in the executive board room at 10:00 a.m."

"OK. Thanks, Bonnie. Did he mention an agenda for the meeting?"

"No, he didn't, Mr. Birkett. He will tell you in the meeting. Thank you. I'll let Mr. Remacle know you'll be there," and without giving Hunter an opportunity to say anything else, she hung up.

At 9:50 a.m., Hunter left his office and went to the elevator. He was curious and at the same time wary, knowing that Remacle never had meetings just to chat.

The door to the boardroom was open, so Hunter walked in. The room was a showpiece, designed to impress, and used whenever a corporate client came to visit. The table was inlaid with teak with the corporate logo embedded in the centre. It seated eighteen people comfortably and each chair was ergonomically designed to conform to the individual who sat in it. The high back made it impossible to see who was sitting in it until you were facing them.

Hunter thought it was an ostentatious waste of money.

When Bonnie had originally called to book the appointment, Hunter had suggested meeting in someplace comfortable. That offer was vetoed quickly, and Hunter knew that booking the boardroom was more about power than anything else.

When Hunter walked into the boardroom, he thought for a moment that he was the first to arrive. He stood in the door for a minute or two pondering what to do and where to sit when finally, the chair closest to the door swiveled around and Mark stood up and extended his hand.

The timing, Hunter knew, was to throw him off balance and knowing this, he smiled and consciously remained in control.

Mark smiled and in a booming voice said, "Hunter, great to see you again. I heard you're married now. Congratulations! How long have you had the old ball and chain?"

Before Hunter had a chance to answer, Mark said, "Sit down and get comfortable. Can I get you anything?"

On the table in front of Mark's chair was a tray with a carafe of coffee, water and an assortment of juices on it.

"Water's good for me. Thanks." Hunter didn't take his eyes off of Mark.

Hunter could see that Mark had his computer set up and it looked like he was working on a project. A manila folder containing papers was positioned next to the computer.

"Hunter, I'm going to get straight to the point. We're thinking of going in a new direction and we think you're the man to get us there. Have you thought about where you want to go to next?"

It wasn't what Hunter had expected and for a moment he was caught off guard.

"Well, yes, I'm interested in moving ahead in my career." Hunter spoke with caution not fully trusting where this was going. "Are we looking at a transfer?"

Hunter knew that the next logical position that he was qualified for above his own was Susan Cannon's.

"No, no transfer. What do you think of Executive VP Sales and Marketing for North America?" Mark was smiling.

It wasn't what Hunter wanted to hear.

"And where would Susan go?" Hunter asked trying to keep his voice neutral so as not to betray how he felt.

"We would be moving Susan to a special project that she is uniquely qualified for." Mark made it sound like Susan would be getting a promotion, but Hunter knew that "special project" would be a way for Mark to minimize her influence.

Hunter was quiet and thought carefully before he spoke. "Have you talked to Susan about this? She has mentored and championed me since I moved to Fixtures and I owe much of my success to her."

For a moment, Mark's façade slipped and a flash of annoyance seemed to cross his face.

"Of course we'll talk to Susan. But we wanted to ascertain your level of interest before we consider going outside the company."

Hunter was torn and confused. He wanted the job. It was a natural progression for him, but his loyalty to his boss and the way this was being positioned didn't sit right with him. From what Mark was saying, Susan was going to be replaced regardless of whether or not he took the position.

"What is the timing of the transition?" Hunter asked.

"We'd like to make this happen as soon as possible," Mark said.

Mark opened the manila folder and picked up a document. It was a contract and the offer for the new position.

"Go ahead. Look it over. I'm sure you'll be happy with what you see," Mark said with confidence.

Hunter noticed that the date they wrote the contract was the day Susan left on her vacation. When he looked at the salary, his eyes widened. It was a substantial increase in pay and had pension, benefits and stock options that were better than he expected.

Hunter thought about how his attitude had changed since he had started to work with Susan Cannon. Less than five years ago, he would have made the decision that put the most money in his pocket. Now he made decisions based on completely new criteria.

His reputation and relationships were now more valuable than the dollar signs he saw in front of him. He wanted the job, but not at any cost.

"I'm interested. And I'm also curious. Our department is doing really well and we can credit Susan with a lot of our success. I have enormous respect for her leadership. Why do you want to move her?"

"We need someone who is strategically placed to move up through the company and take on more leadership roles. Susan has let us know that she wants to wind down her career." Mark stated this as if it was common knowledge and a matter of fact.

Hunter knew Susan well and he had never heard her talk about winding down her career. Hunter's gut told him there was something else at play.

"When do you need my answer?" Hunter asked.

"How about if I give you a call in a week? Talk it over with your new wife. I can answer any other questions you have at that time."

Mark stood up and smiled at Hunter. The meeting was over.

"I need you on my team, Hunter. I hope you'll see the opportunity I'm giving you. When I look at you, I see a man I can identify with. Someone who is just like me."

Hunters lips narrowed and a crease appeared between his eyes. He did not think Mark actually knew him at all, and he certainly didn't want to be "just like" Mark.

Hunter realized he was being dismissed and extended his hand. "Thanks for the opportunity. I'll talk to you next week."

Mark looked smug. When Hunter was gone, Mark picked up the phone and called his friend Ed Southern.

"Ed, thanks for the lowdown on Hunter Birkett. No one seemed to know about the business with his last company; otherwise, I can't imagine that the big suits would have okayed his hire. He's exactly what I need on my team and I'm pretty sure he'll take the offer. I know how to handle his type." Those words would come back to haunt Mark.

It was close to lunch when Hunter walked back to his office and his mind was in turmoil. He sat down, remembered the heart, body mind technique, and used it to gather his thoughts. He made a decision.

"Louise, cancel any other meetings today. I'll be working from home."

When he jumped into his car to drive home, the light rain from the morning had turned into a downpour. The wipers furiously tried to keep up, the drive had a few white-knuckle moments as inexperienced drivers hydroplaned, and he didn't see the car that was stalled until he was almost on it. He yanked the wheel to avoid hitting it.

He hit the curb and cursed when he heard the crunch. When he stepped out to look at the damage, his heart sank. The tire was bent inward and the car would have to be towed. He waited an hour for the tow truck to come and another half an hour to get a ride home. He wasn't sure he could deal with any more stress, but he knew if the situation were reversed, Susan would do everything she could to reach him, so he sucked it up.

Hunter walked in the door to the condo and searched until he found the information on how Susan could be reached in case of an emergency. He decided that this meeting with Mark qualified.

Susan was on a cruise ship sailing through the Panama Canal. Getting a message to her was difficult but not impossible. He had the name of the cruise line and the ship.

Hunter called the 800 number that patched him to the ship by satellite link. The call was directed to the Purser on board who took the information and said that he would page Susan and get the message to her as soon as possible.

While he waited, he went over the morning meeting with Mark. The more he thought about it, the more Hunter's choice became clear. He wouldn't work for Mark.

If there was just one thing Hunter had learned in the last year: Trust was at the core of any good business relationship, but Mark was a player, not a leader.

He felt disappointment since he had believed Fixtures actually was a different kind of company. But if they chose Mark to lead the company, then maybe Hunter had misjudged Fixtures… or maybe he was wrong about Mark?

He knew Susan was different, but maybe she was the exception at Fixtures. The honest person in a dishonest world. Hunter was so deep in these dark thoughts, that when the phone rang, he literally jumped. He saw it was Susan calling from her cell.

"Hello?"

"Hunter, what's up? I've got about half an hour before I leave the ship to explore the Gamboa Rain forest. If I miss the tender to shore, I'm stuck on board the ship with the buffet people.'"" Susan sounded surprised to hear from him.

"Mark Remacle called me in to a meeting and I'm pretty sure he timed it thinking I wouldn't be able to talk to you." Hunter sounded grim.

"Mark?" Susan said with an edge to her voice, "Now what's he up to?"

"Susan, are you planning early retirement and forgot to tell me?"

"What!!" Susan laughed. "As much as I'm enjoying this holiday, I'm not ready to quit my job just yet. What's going on?"

Hunter gave Susan the details about his meeting with Remacle.

"It sounds like quite a good offer, Hunter. What are you feeling?" Susan stopped speaking for a moment and he could hear her talk to someone on the ship. "Sorry for the interruption. I had to let them know I'll take the last tender to shore. So?"

"In the past four years I've learned what it's like to work with people I trust and respect. I know what it feels like to be trusted. So I'll cut to the chase: I'm not going to work for Mark no matter what he offers or threatens."

"I was hoping you'd feel that way, because something is definitely off in this. Let me call around and I promise I'll call you as soon as I find out more. Are you okay with that?"

Susan's cell phone started to beep.

"I'm going to lose you soon. My cell phone is going to die. I'll call you..."

When Susan's cell phone died, Hunter still had many questions to ask her. He wanted to figure out what they were going to do while maintaining integrity and their own self-respect.

The thing was, while Hunter didn't want to work for Mark, he also didn't want to have some kind of showdown. Especially since Hunter knew that not that long ago, he'd acted a lot like Mark.

"There but for the grace of God go I," he said quietly to himself.

This realization led Hunter to think of all the leaders he'd worked with. Some didn't deserve that title, some really did. He wrote out a list to see the differences.

REAL LEADERS

- Pulls everyone in, values us for real.
- Gives opportunities, takes risk for us.
- Talks about the POINT of what we're doing.
- Shows us a vision that we can follow.
- Keeps promises.
- Does real work, not just blah blah.
- Actually LISTENS, not just fake it.
- Enjoys being with us.
- Excited about our success.

- Pushes us to risk, grow, try.
- Tells us what we're doing right... and wrong.
- Challenges self – and us.
- Connected to us, even knows our families.
- Shows us we're valued – not just perks, but really personally.
- Walks the talk. Real apologies when makes mistakes.
- Someone you wish you could introduce to your mom, "Hey, this is my boss, he's a rockstar" – and actually mean it.

FAKE LEADERS

- Focused on self, own rep.
- Tells what to do, not why.
- Vague, unclear, unspecific communication.
- Only interested in us agreeing, shuts down challenges.
- Distant (call it "professional" but really no caring)
- Plays favorites.
- Tells us what we are doing wrong, never what we are doing right.
- Says one thing, does another.
- Pretends to listen.
- Doesn't really give credit... or totally general.
- Dumps extra work on us as "normal."
- Doesn't really KNOW each of us.
- Not self aware. Doesn't even realize when being a jack###.
- No sincere apologies. Not much sincere anything, actually.

When he completed the list, he thought he'd ask A.J. to look it over and give him feedback and see if he had missed anything.

He looked outside and could see the rain had not let up. It was now a solid sheet of rain and he was worried about A.J. driving home. She was late, so he picked up the phone.

A.J. answered immediately, "Hunter, I'm stuck and I'm scared. I can't believe you just called. I was looking for my phone. I don't know what to do. I skidded off the road and I'm in the ditch. The door is pushed in against the seatbelt and I can't unbuckle it. I can't get out of the car. Come and get me."

Hunter had never heard A.J. so panicked and his heart started to race.

"A.J., where are you?" Hunter kept his voice calm.

A.J. gave him the directions the best she could. It was now getting dark. A.J. had been working at a community school outside of the city and was driving on a lonely stretch of road when she lost control and hit the ditch.

"I had a fender bender and my car is in the shop but don't worry, I'll call a tow truck and they'll have you out of there in no time. With our luck maybe we should buy shares in a towing operation!"

Hunter was trying to lighten her worry with humor, but A.J. didn't laugh.

"Don't worry, sweetheart. You'll be home before you know it. Stay on the phone and I'll call a towing company on my cell," Hunter said reassuringly.

Hunter called every towing company in the region and nothing was available. He even called a taxi company offering them an extra hundred and fifty on top of the fare if they would drive out.

"Sorry mister. You could offer a thousand and fifty and we couldn't drive out there. There isn't a taxi available."

Hunter was in a panic. He picked up the phone to A.J., who had been able to hear a one sided conversation.

"You need to come get me now. I'm in a ditch and I can feel water on my feet so the ditch must be filling with water."

Hunter had never felt so powerless.

"A.J., don't worry. I'll get you out. "

Hunter knew that the calm he had worked so hard to maintain was gone. His voice mirrored the concern he was feeling.

"I'm going to hang up. Don't worry. I'll be there as soon as I can. I'll call you when I'm on my way." Hunter called the only person that he knew he could rely on, no matter what.

When Rick Phillips answered the phone and heard what Hunter had to say, he didn't hesitate for a moment. He was at Hunter's home within five minutes and they were on their way to find A.J.

Rick had a truck that had seen better days, but it had the power to get through anything. Hunter dialed A.J.

"Where are you! The water is up to the seat. I'm scared, Hunter. I'm scared. Where are you?"

"We're on our way. Hang on. It's going to take us another five minutes to get to you. I'll stay on with you. When we get close, I want you to start honking the horn. Make sure the lights are on. We need to be able to find you."

"OK. Hurry Hunter. I'm sitting in water now and it's cold. I don't know how long I can handle this," her voice cracked.

He tried to keep A.J. from panicking, but it was a losing battle for both of them. He needed to do something, but he was totally powerless. It was the longest five minutes of Hunters life. "Ok, A.J. Honk the horn. Keep honking the horn."

In the distance, Hunter and Rick could hear the faint sound of a horn. As Rick drove along the road, it got louder and both Hunter and Rick were encouraged.

Then A.J.'s phone died and Hunter literally felt his own heart dropping as fear started overtaking his whole body.

Rick was the one who saw the faint lights in the ditch.

"I see something! Look! Can you see it?" Rick spoke with nervous excitement.

"I don't see anything! Where? Where?" Hunter didn't realize he was shouting.

Rick sped up and stopped beside a faint light that was glowing at the side of the road.

Hunter jumped out of the car into the pouring rain and ran to the ditch. He saw A.J.s car partially submerged. The water was half way up the door.

Hunter jumped into the ditch and tried to open the door. The weight of the water and the damaged door made it impossible to open. It was so dark that he couldn't see inside the car but he knew that A.J. was inside and he was frantic.

Rick reached into his back seat – he'd brought his carpenter's bag. He reached in, grabbed a hammer, and handed it to Hunter.

Hunter gripped the hammer and with one quick hit, he took out the back window on the driver's side.

Hunter climbed through the shattered glass, not even noticing if he cut himself. A.J. was shivering badly and she smiled weakly when she saw him.

Hunter tried to reach down to unlock the seatbelt but it wouldn't budge.

"Rick, hand me a blade, anything that will cut through this seatbelt!" Hunter yelled through the open window.

He turned and smiled at A.J. "Don't worry, sweetheart, I'll chew through it if I have to."

Hunter didn't know where he got the strength, but once he cut the seatbelt, he lifted A.J. up and over the back seat and out through the window.

Hunter wrapped A.J. in the blankets they had brought. "We're going to take you to the hospital to get checked out."

Rick drove as fast as he safely could and reached the hospital in record time. Hunter just wrapped himself around A.J. and buried his face in her wet hair, both of them shaking with cold and fear.

The heat in the cab of the truck was turned up full, and by the time they reached the hospital, A.J. was telling them they were over reacting and she just wanted to go home for a warm bath. The shivering was subsiding and she managed a smile.

It took a lot of convincing but they turned the truck and headed for home.

The rain was still heavy when Rick dropped Hunter and A.J. off.

"How can I ever repay you, Rick? I owe you my life!" Hunter whispered.

Rick smiled, "Yeah... I'll collect later."

The rain continued to fall.

CHAPTER 7

RICH AND TRUSTED – SEEING TRUST IN ACTION

T he next day, Hunter thought about how much he now trusted Rick. The bonds of friendship that Hunter had shredded were now tightly woven back together. Hunter realized he really did mean what he'd said to Rick, he felt like he owed the man his life. Partly for being the kind of guy who'd think to bring his tool bag, but even more for the whole way he'd responded. Trust combines character and competence in equal measure.

Hunter and A.J. called in and let their offices know they wouldn't be into work. The rain continued to fall and now both of them were without vehicles. Taxis were almost impossible to secure and besides, after dual car accidents, they both figured it was a good day to just stay inside.

Hunter called the car rental; The only two available were a large van and a luxury car. "At least you can be really stylish," Hunter joked. But underneath A.J. could see his tenderness and concern. The 'what if's' that crowded his mind made him physically feel weak. He closed his eyes, and put his head in his hands and said a silent thank you.

When he opened his eyes, he saw the list of leadership dos and don'ts he had written the day before. It seemed a lifetime ago; he hadn't even told A.J. about the meeting with Mark Remacle. For the next hour, he filled her in on all that happened.

"This whole business with Mark makes me feel uncomfortable. I never felt like he was giving me the straight goods. There were hidden meanings and sub texts to every word that came out of his mouth. He had a hidden agenda." Hunter was thoughtful as he spoke.

"For the past four and a half years you've worked with a straight talker. Susan thinks about what she says and demonstrates a genuine care for everyone who works for her. She respects all of you. Could you really work with someone of Mark's character?" A.J. asked.

"Are you okay supporting me if this doesn't work out?" Hunter smiled, but the worry showed in his eyes.

A.J.'s answer was a hug and a kiss.

The TV announcement caught their attention. Hunter turned up the volume.

"Heavy rains continue to fall and officials warn of potential flooding and damage to property. Department of the Environment is working closely with civic officials to monitor river levels and people are advised to check flood warnings in their region. Emergency crews have been working around the clock. A record rainfall was recorded at Pearson International. Flights have been cancelled. Travelers are advised to call and confirm before heading to the airport." The announcer went on to give a list of emergency numbers to call and agencies to contact.

"A.J., Rick and his family live in the new subdivision that backs on to the river. I'm going to give him a call and see how he's doing." Hunter reached for the phone.

The phone rang four times and went into voice mail.

"Of course, he's probably at work." Hunter looked perplexed.

A.J. said, "I'm surprised that Anna isn't at home. She's not working. Try Rick's cell."

The phone was picked up on the first ring. The call display let Rick know who was calling.

"Hunter' I can't talk. I need to keep this line free and I'm afraid I'm going to run out of battery power." Rick Phillips sounded anxious and out of breath.

"Rick, what's happening?" In the twenty years Hunter had known Rick, he had never heard him sound like this. Rick was the guy that stayed calm when everyone else was losing their heads. Now he sounded panicked and worried.

"Our basement is completely flooded and the water keeps rising. We've lost power. I can't believe how quickly this happened. I've been trying to get through to emergency services." Rick was shouting to be heard over the sound of the rushing water.

"Hang on. Give me the number and I'll keep calling and get help for you. Stay off the phone. I'll call back as soon as I can." Hunter hung up the phone and turned to A.J.

"Do you remember the numbers that they gave on the newscast?" Hunter spoke quickly.

"No, but I'll check on the computer."A.J. went over to computer and within minutes, she had the numbers for Hunter to call.

Hunter called every number that was listed and got either a busy signal or a message from a beleaguered person who told them that the best that could be done was to take the information and send out a crew when one was available.

It felt like hours since he had talked to Rick, but only 30 minutes had elapsed since the first call.

Rick picked up his phone on the first ring.

"What's happening? Who's coming? Our basement is completely flooded." Rick spoke rapidly. Hunter could hear a child crying in the background.

"You need to get the family out of there. Can you safely drive?"

"No. I looked outside and we are now part of the lake."

"OK We're calling in the troops," Hunter said. "I'll call you back,"

"A.J., what's the name of the…" Hunter paused searching his memory. "Crap… what is it called? RAP, RART… you know, the military branch that rescues people?"

"I think it's called DART. I'll check on the computer." A.J. was gone for less than a minute.

"Yup, it's called DART for Disaster Assistance Response Team and the number is 905-555-3278. It's a Kingston number."

"Blast, don't they have anything closer? That's three hours away!" Hunter's voice rose.

"Hunter, they're probably already here. Call! Find out, and for God's sake, breathe!"

When he called, he was relieved to hear that they had already sent out troops to help with the flood victims. The DART team was sent anywhere and everywhere in the world they were needed, to crises ranging from natural disasters to complex humanitarian emergencies.

A logistics platoon had been deployed earlier to determine what was needed. They coordinated the rest of the troops and brought in whatever equipment was needed. Boats, heavy equipment and troops to provide the muscle were already at work.

The military personnel officer assured Hunter that Rick and his family would be safe and on dry land within the hour.

Hunter called back and tried to send reassurance through the phone lines. He knew that the rescue operations would be tricky. He had the TV on and he could see the military maneuvering boats through waters that were littered with debris.

Another three hours lapsed before he heard back from his friend.

"Hello."

The worry Hunter had been feeling could be heard in the tightness of his voice and could be seen with the white-knuckle grip on his phone.

"We're all safe. I can't talk long. I'm on someone else's phone. We're at the Red Cross Centre on Queen Street."

Rick sounded exhausted. The strain of being on high alert was gone and the complex cocktail of stress hormones had left his system, draining him of the last of his energy. He was hit with the reality of not having a home to go to.

"I'll be there in twenty minutes. You're all coming here. You can stay as long as you need. We have two extra bedrooms and A.J. has cooked a hot meal for all of you. Besides, I owe you one. I didn't think I'd be able to do the payback so soon." Hunter was relieved and grateful that his friend and his family were okay.

He had already talked it over with A.J. and she was as insistent as Hunter that the family come and stay with them.

Hunter could hear Rick talking to Anna. "Thanks Hunter... and thank A.J. We're grateful."

Hunter jumped in the van and drove towards Queen St. The street was barricaded and the military and the Red Cross had set up tents and a triage centre to handle those who had been left homeless from the flooding.

He walked another three blocks before he was able to find them. The huddled clusters of people all appeared the same. Grey with mud smudged faces, they looked sad and forlorn.

Rick saw Hunter and called out, "Hunter, we're over here! OK everyone, Uncle Hunter is here. Let's get going."

Rick's youngest daughter was five years old and didn't seem in the least bit worried about the situation. She was sitting on Anna's lap studying Hunter with the innocent intensity of a bright child who had listened in on too many adult conversations.

"I don't have an Uncle Hunter. And Mama said she's willing to be wrong about Hunter. Is that you? What does that mean?"

Anna looked appalled. "Chrissie! That's enough." Anna's cheek flushed and she looked down.

"Chrissie, it means that your Mama has a forgiving heart. Now how about if I give you a piggy back and we go to my house for a sleep over." Hunter smiled kindly at Anna as he scooped up Chrissie.

Rick's ten-year-old son was trying to show Hunter how brave he was. His streak lined face showed the fright and fears of the last 10 hours but he managed a weak smile. Rick reached over and tenderly put his hand on his son's head.

Without another word being spoken, they got up and followed Hunter to the van.

When they got to the condo, A.J. opened the door before anyone had a chance to. She swept Anna into an embrace and said, "La mia casa è la vostra casa. Che cosa ho è inoltre i vostri. My house is your house. What I have is also yours."

Anna wept.

While A.J. got Anna and the children set up in their rooms, Hunter and Rick had an opportunity to talk in the living room.

"Will your insurance take care of the flooding, Rick?" Hunter asked.

"It would if we lived in the States and I could afford to buy the extra policy." Rick laughed ironically. "I couldn't get flood insurance for our house. We're covered by the government's disaster financial assistance. And I'm not sure if it covers the contents of our house. If it doesn't, I don't know how we're going to make it." Rick put his head in his hands.

The next morning, Hunter woke up with the germ of a plan. In a whispered morning conversation, A.J. told he was taking too much on.

"Hunter, it's enough that you have to figure out what you're doing with the Mark Remacle offer. Your job has enough stress. I love that you want to do this but where are you going to find the time?"

When he got to the office, he saw a message from A.J. letting him know she was taking Rick and family to Anna's mom's place.

"Louise, I'm putting my calls directly into voice mail for the next hour. If anyone comes by, can you let them know I'm not to be disturbed? I'll fill you in when I'm done. There's a lot to tell!"

With a clear mind, he started putting together a marketing plan. The goal was to raise money for the people who were affected by the flood, starting with Rick and his family. For a solid two hours, he put his head down and worked.

In a week, his life had been turned upside down. The flood of rain mirrored the flood of emotions that had been pelting him for the past four days.

His cell rang and broke his reverie. It was Susan. Time to find out what was happening with his future.

"Hunter, it's Susan. I've been trying to reach you the past couple of days. Is everything OK?"

Traveling through the Panama Canal, news from home was practically non-existent in the floating bubble of a cruise ship.

"How much time do you have?" Hunter asked with seriousness.

"Wow... this does sound ominous. We only have half an hour. I know that's not much but we'll be docking in two days and I'll be home in three. Can it wait until I get home? This sounds like a sit down conversation and I'd like to give you my full attention."

"Yeah, actually I think that's best. There's no way I could tell you all of what has happened in half an hour. In a nutshell, there was a flood, I've got a plan and I'll need you to sign off on some volunteer time for me and some of my staff for the next couple of days. Are you OK with that?"

"Wow, that's quite a lead in. Hunter, it's killing me not to ask what's going on but I know I'll find out when I get back. Go ahead. I trust you and you've got my approval."

Susan's voice changed when she starting talking about Mark. It was something he'd rarely heard from her, but there was definitely a sharp edge.

"I'd like to fill you in on what I know about Mark and my new 'special assignment.'"

Apparently, because Susan had challenged Mark in a couple of high level meetings, the staff shuffle was Mark's gambit to get someone he felt he could control. Where Susan was transparent and let people know that what you saw was what you got, Mark had a hidden agenda and ruled for the perceived power that the title and position gave him. He had a brilliant mind but a feeble soul.

What Mark didn't know was that Susan enjoyed a warm relationship with John Pitt and his family. Very few in the company knew that both John's father-in-law and Susan's father were both afflicted with Alzheimer's. John's wife and Susan had met in the doctor's office a couple of years before and had become allies in that terrible struggle. The friendship was not common knowledge because Susan would never use her personal relationship to further her career at work. It was only one of the many key differences between Mark and Susan.

"So, I've got a week to decide what I'm going to do and so do you. In the meantime, do your volunteer work."

"Right Susan, I will. And I have a feeling about this thing with Mark. It's all going to work out just fine."

Hunter knew that while the politics would be messy, and the Mark-mess could kill his career, it just didn't seem as important today. He walked out of his office to Louise's desk.

"Louise, I'm setting up a meeting in the upstairs executive boardroom for one thirty. I'm putting together a fundraiser and this is not an obligatory meeting, but it's open if you'd like to be there as well." Hunter smiled at Louis and got back to his desk to keep preparing.

Hunter emailed a bunch of good Fixtures people inviting them to join him at one thirty if they were interested in working on a fundraiser. Hunter gave enough information so that people would know what it was for, but left it open enough so he could explain more when they arrived.

The rain had stopped and water levels were starting to recede. Pictures of the damage were all over the news. For the next couple of weeks, people would be interested in helping out before the next disaster struck and the mood and heart of the public shifted. If Hunter wanted to get help for the victims of the flood, he knew he had to act fast.

Hunter called and spoke to the General Manager of the largest venue in town. The Rogers Centre was formerly called the SkyDome and would comfortably hold over twenty thousand people. Within two weeks, Hunter wanted to stage a benefit concert with all of the money raised going to a special fund to support people who were affected by the flood.

By the time 1:30 rolled around, Hunter had the skeleton of a plan. What would normally take months to put together was going to be done in two weeks. It was a monumental task and he needed people who were willing to put in the work to get it done.

All of Hunter's team showed up looking curious. About a dozen other people had also responded to the call for action.

"Some of you have workloads that are pretty crazy, so if it's not possible for you to take on any more work, let me know before we get started. For those of you who work for me, I want you to know that this is a volunteer assignment and I don't want anyone to feel they have to sign up."

A couple of people on his team excused themselves and looked relieved. Hunter knew that they were tapped out and he thought no less of them for leaving.

"In the past week each of us has been touched by the tragedies and heart wrenching personal stories and like me, many of you know people who have been devastated by the flood. Lives have been lost and homes have been destroyed."

He stopped and looked as people nodded to each other. He could see that a couple of them had tears in their eyes as they thought of family and friends who were homeless because of the floods. The words had an effect because Hunter spoke from the heart.

"I'm going to ask something of each of you that will take up all of your spare time. In every life, there is a moment when we are asked to make a difference. Something that captures our heart and soul and tells us that with hard work, dedication and determination we can help make a life better."

Hunter paused and let what he was asking of them sink in.

"We're going to put on a benefit concert with a hundred percent of the funds raised going to the people who need it the most. I've got a list of over a hundred families that have been left homeless as a result of the flood. Families who lost all of their personal items and don't have a bed to sleep in. We are going to raise enough money to get them back on their feet."

He hit a button on his computer and a picture of the Rogers Centre came into view.

"Two weeks from now we are going to fill this stadium. I've started working on a plan to bring in top acts from across Canada to put on a concert. Each of you have skills that we need. If your brain is telling you that it can't be done, I want you to ignore it and listen to your heart. But if you want to get up and leave now, I completely understand."

No one moved.

"OK. Let's get started. For those of you who are working for Fixtures, you can use this charity work as your paid week of volunteer time. For all of you I can promise you long hours, crappy coffee and cold pizza."

Hunter looked around the room and smiled. He counted twenty four people. Eight of them from his staff and another ten were people from other departments who at one time or another had done projects with him and his team. A small minority were from outside of the company. Each volunteer was asked to find and build a team, because they would need over five hundred volunteers to put the show together.

By the end of the hour, people had been assigned tasks and a project plan with him at the helm had been hammered out.

All it took was one big name to get the ball rolling. A friend knew a senior officer in the RCMP whose son was a major film star.

Hunter called and did some of the best selling of his whole career. Once the star agreed to host the show, the rest of the big names seemed to fall in place. Before long, Hunter was fielding calls from bands that were begging to be part of the show. When an international circus offered to do a set from their latest show, Hunter found a way to make it happen.

The logistics of getting lighting, sound, advertising, and production arranged was a twenty four hour job and Hunter still had to find time to manage his job. Hunter was awake at 5:00 a.m. and never got to bed before midnight.

When Susan got back to the office two days later, she saw a hub of activity and very little of it had to do with work. People were laughing and shouting the names of stars who were going to be part of the show. The energy was infectious.

"I can see that you've been obsessing about Mark and the decision you need to make," Susan smiled sardonically.

"What?" Hunter was looking at a list of things that needed to be done for the concert. It took him a minute to refocus and think about work.

"Right. I told Mark I would get back to him with a decision." The tiredness he had been holding off grabbed at him when he thought about what he had to do.

"I've worked really hard to be the man that deserves A.J. and is a model for Laura. I'm not stepping back into the guy who walked in the door four and a half years ago. I've talked it over with A.J. and we can manage until I get another job. I'm tendering my resignation." Hunter's voice sounded as tired as he felt.

"Well Hunter, you won't be alone. When you first mentioned retirement, I laughed, but the idea has grown on me. If I take early retirement, I can spend time with my Dad while he still knows who I am." Susan put her hand on Hunter's shoulder. "It's been a pleasure working with you, Hunter."

"You as well, Susan. I'll look for a good reference from you. I'll need it."

THE BIG SHOW

Putting together a big concert is supposed to take months of hard work. Putting it together in two weeks is akin to building a house in that same two week time frame. It can be done, but there's a lot of craziness and it usually ends up that there are some rooms that don't have a door. The team that Hunter had working for him was dedicated and would do anything he asked of them. He made sure that everyone took care of themselves and took time off, but he worked an impossible schedule and only ate and slept when A.J. insisted.

By the day of the "Time for Trust Concert," they had built not a house, but a cathedral. The concert was telecast internationally and a phone bank was set up to take donations. In the first hour, they passed their original $one million goal, and the final tally was well over five million dollars.

A charity had been set up to help the families who were left homeless because of a disaster. It bridged the gap when people were without funds and waiting for help and helped support families until they got on their feet. With the funds from the concert, "The Rainy Day Foundation" was able to support thousands of families.

"You've given us our lives back," Rick said to Hunter. It was a comment he heard often.

Hunter was asked to serve on the board. He knew that what they had started would continue to grow and help people for many, many years. It was quite a paradox for Hunter to see how he'd helped all these people get their lives together, while his career was about to fall apart – again.

THE TERMINATION LETTER

When Hunter had asked, Remacle had given an extra week for Hunter to decide on the promotion to Executive VP... and taking over Susan's job. Most likely Mark's patience had been fueled by the good press about the concert, and the fact that Fixtures' staff were the key organizers. The event unintentionally gave a positive glow to everyone in the company.

Naturally, Mark took as much credit as he could by telling people that he was the one who'd given Hunter and the others time for such an important cause.

Still, a glow only lasts so long, and Hunter's time was up. On the day he had to give his answer, Hunter woke up early and lay in bed, listening to the sounds of the house and A.J.'s soft snores (that she firmly denied).

By 6:30, he was up, showered and changed and the coffee was made. He was ready to walk out the door by 7:00.

Before he left, Hunter looked at A.J. and smiled. "Are you ready to be the sole breadwinner for awhile?"

A.J. put her arms around Hunter and gave him a hug. "I will be there to support you as long as you need it," and with a laugh she added, "but I've already arranged a dishwashing job for you at Umberto's!"

Hunter looked at his wife. "You know A.J., these past five years have taught me so much. I've learned what trust is from Susan and even more, what love and trust are from you. I'm not worried about what happens. I said it to Susan that I just know everything is going to be okay."

A.J. put her arms around and her husband and hugged him tight. "I'm proud of you. Call me as soon as you've given HR your letter."

As usual, Hunter was one of the first to arrive at the company. He went into his office and looked around. It looked a lot different than the first day he had arrived. Pictures on his desk and credenza showed family, friends and coworkers laughing and enjoying life. It was the desk of a well-loved and respected leader.

He pulled out the envelope with the carefully worded letter that he had written. He was going to call Mark and verbally let him know his decision. In addition, he had made an appointment with HR to hand in the formal letter.

1-905-555-1222
Hunter.Birkett@Fixtures.org
Mrs. Susan Cannon
Executive VP Marketing – FixturesToronto, Ontario,

Dear Ms. Cannon,

I am writing to announce my resignation from Fixtures, effective immediately.

This was not an easy decision to make on my part. The past five years have been very rewarding. I've enjoyed managing a successful team dedicated to marketing the products and creating success in the marketplace for Fixtures.

Thank you for the opportunities for growth that have been provided for me. I can say unequivocally that I have grown as a person because of working for you.

I wish the company continued success.

Sincerely,

Hunter Birkett
Hunter Birkett
VP Marketing

He waited until Louise was in the office and called her in. He knew that she would be upset and he didn't want her hearing it from anyone else but him.

"Louise, I've enjoyed working with you and I've appreciated you making me look good for the past five years." Hunter poured a glass of water and readied the Kleenex.

"What do you mean, Mr. Birkett? You're not leaving, are you?" Louise looked at him with concern.

Hunter showed her the letter. When the tears started flowing, he pushed the Kleenex across the desk and handed her a glass of water. He knew Louise and wasn't surprised by her show of tears.

"Mr. Birkett, I've never worked for a better boss. Where are you going?" Louise's eyes were red and she was working hard to calm herself.

"I'm going to take some time off to decide that Louise. My wife A.J. and I may do some traveling. Who knows? You need to keep this under wraps until HR is informed. Can you do that for me?" Hunter smiled warmly at Louise.

When Louise left his office, Hunter walked over to Susan's office and knocked on the door. The door was open and she was waiting for him.

"Come on in and close the door. You look like a man on a mission." Susan smiled warmly.

Hunter handed Susan the letter.

"I'm actually quite excited about what the future holds for me. I've been asked to sit on a couple of boards of small startup companies. At least I'll be pulling in some revenue... although I don't imagine it will be a lot to begin with. The potential is pretty amazing."

Susan looked at Hunter. "Well, you could still sit on those boards even if you continued to work here. As long as there is no conflict of interest, there wouldn't be a problem."

Hunter looked surprised.

Susan continues, "Hunter, I handed in my letter of resignation last week. Like I told you, I want to spend time with my father.

Financially I don't need to work and I can't imagine anyone else but you taking over my position when I'm gone."

"Susan, we've talked about this. I'm not taking your job and reporting to Mark Remacle."

There was a moment of silence before she continued.

"Hunter, I was in an awkward position. Of course, I recommend you but I also knew that you would be resigning. I know John and his wife personally, so I was frank with him and explained that you would be tendering your resignation as well. That's all I am allowed to tell you, but I want you to trust me, on faith and without asking questions that I can't answer at this time. Take back your letter and take the promotion. It will all work out. You'll see."

Hunter started to ask questions but Susan cut him off.

"I'm asking you to take a leap of faith. Look at the almost five years we've worked together and just… well, just take the damn promotion."

Hunter walked back to his office and called Louise in to ask her discretion and not to mention it to anyone else. He said that Susan has asked him to reconsider and he was taking the rest of the day off to decide.

Louise looked pleased and relieved.

He called A.J. When she saw his number come up, she answered immediately.

"How are you doing? What did HR say? Is everyone in shock? Did you talk to Mark Remacle yet? What did he say?" A.J. didn't pause between any of her questions, so Hunter didn't have a chance to respond.

"A.J., A.J. slow down. Well… it didn't exactly go as planned. Susan has asked me to reconsider and take her position. I'm going to take the rest of the day off. What's your schedule like? Can you meet me for a walk?"

"WHAT!? Seriously? Wow, this is a curve ball." A.J. sounded as shocked as Hunter felt. "Yeah, I'll see you at the park in half an hour."

When Hunter and A.J. met, he shared Susan's mysterious story.

"In my mind there is no question. You know Susan wouldn't ask something like this if it would be a bad move for you," A.J. said with conviction. "Besides, let me ask you... If Mark wasn't in the picture, would you accept the job?"

"In a heartbeat! I love the people I work with and the job challenges me in more ways than even my own company did."

"Then you don't need the rest of the afternoon. Call Susan and let her know now."

Hunter called Susan. She congratulated him, and said to call Mark Remacle and accept the promotion. She pushed him to do it right away.

Hunter was nervous calling Mark. He felt like he might be stepping on a land mine, so he kept it short and professional, accepting the position of Executive VP and thanking him for the opportunity. He swallowed hard and bit his tongue when Mark said he was glad to have someone who finally thought like him and would carry out his plans.

THE NEW POSITION

The next day Hunter was at his desk early, as always. In the quiet, he kept wondering if he had made the right decision. Still "Executive VP" had a nice ring to it.

By 8:00, he was walking down the hall to Susan's office. She was already sitting at her desk and looked up and smiled when she heard him in her doorway.

"Hunter, John Pitt made me promise not to say anything until you had formally accepted the position and it was all approved and tied up with a bow. HR pushed through the paperwork quickly and you are officially Senior Vice President of Sales and Marketing for North America."

Hunter started to correct her about the job title, but Susan held up a finger to stop him.

"There will be a memo going out in a few minutes about the reorg in our senior leadership. As of today, you're reporting directly into the President, John Pitt."

Hunter's mouth opened and shut. "And what about Mark Remacle?"

"Well, it seems that John had been waiting for just one more piece of evidence that Mark wasn't aligned with the company values. I believe that when faced with the choice of leaving or shifting, Mark volunteered to take on those same special projects he was going to give me."

Hunter was quiet for a moment and then said, "Okay Susan, but you should be the SVP, I'd be thrilled to keep reporting to you."

Susan got up from her chair and motioned for him to sit down.

"I apologize for sitting in your chair, Mr. Birkett. Officially, as of 5:00 p.m. yesterday, I am retired!"

Susan stood up, moved behind her chair, and pointed to it.

Hunter smiled and shook his head. "Susan, if I've learned anything from you it's that important conversations don't need to happen when you're sitting behind a desk. Can I invite you to take a comfortable seat?"

Both Hunter and Susan walked over and each sat in a comfortable chair facing each other. They talked about the new role, and how to manage the reorg, and a hundred practical details. As the conversation was winding down, Hunter looked seriously at Susan.

"Susan, I want to say thank you again for the chance you gave me. But what you really did was help me find direction when I didn't have any."

Susan tried to wave away the compliment, but Hunter continued. "Do you remember when we talked about noble goals? I don't think I ever told you what I decided. Ny noble goal is 'To nurture trust.' For the rest of my life it will be a compass that guides me."

Susan had a tear in her eye. "Hunter, you know what, it's a great trade. Because watching you rebuild your relationship with your kid, and fall in love with A.J. – well the way you've been dedicated to those people helped me decide to do some things I've always wanted to do. I'm going to spend time and travel and just be with my dad. And knowing my department is in good hands, it gives me the courage to step into this next adventure."

Susan stood up. "It's time for me to start my retirement. I'd wish you luck but you won't need it."

She walked over, gave Hunter a hug, turned, and walked out the door.

When Susan left, Hunter went and sat at his new desk. Susan had taken her belongings, but she left one item, the sign that he had noticed the first day when he started working at Fixtures.

Trust:

The willingness to accept vulnerability based

upon positive expectations about

another's behavior.

He decided to walk back to his old office and move in. But while he'd been talking to Susan, the memo had gone out. For the second time in his career at Fixtures, people stood up and clapped as he walked by. This time Hunter wasn't in a track suit.

When he got to his old office, he sat down at his desk drinking in all that had happened. He reached for the phone to call his wife. Before he had a chance to call her, the phone rang. He could see that it was A.J. calling him.

"Hey, I was just going to call you. You won't believe what happened."

"Me first! Hunter, you remember those Community Hero awards we saw last year?" A.J.'s voice was full of pride and love and just a little teasing. "You won't believe who they nominated for their top award this year!"

Hunter laughed, "I hope we can trust they know what they're doing!"

Professional Speaker and Author, Lea Brovedani started her career as a receptionist at a small head-hunting firm in Calgary. Within two years, she was managing a branch office in Denver. She learned to build powerful, trust-based relationships with clients, but when the head office decided to close all of the branch offices, it wasn't long before the business closed down and Lea was unemployed. She took a leap of faith, trusting her great clients, and started her own company. She learned what it takes to grow and thrive in a down economy.

Lea met Ric just before he left for Africa. She decided to trust her heart, so she stepped away from her business to join him. When they landed in Egypt, they discovered the beauty of the Red Sea and the wonder of diving. Determined not to be left behind, Lea quickly learned how to swim, and then dive. From shore to deep sea was another lesson in trust – she learned how to take the right risks.

While she was raising her young family, Lea decided she needed to challenge herself (as if raising two rambunctious kids wasn't enough). She set her sights on the New York Marathon. She learned that trusting in your own hard work could get you to the finish line, a lesson that has served her well in all her endeavors.

For the past 15 years, Lea has advised and inspired clients across Asia, Europe, and North America to improve trust in the workplace.

Fearless inside and outside the classroom, Lea has gone scuba diving with sharks, skydiving, bungy jumping and zip lining. When someone asked her if she had a death wish her reply was "I don't... I have a life wish." Lea brings her joy of life onto the stage and into the classroom to present programs that transform thinking and show people how to increase trust in their businesses and their daily lives.

Trust has been a recurring theme throughout her life, but she's learned you can't push trust, you have to tell the story and invite people in. TRUSTED is a work of love, and a story of invaluable lessons for all of us as leaders and leaders of our lives.

To contact Lea to speak at your event or arrange training for your organization go to www.leabrovedani.com or email her at: lea.brovedani@6seconds.org.

You can also contact her through the Six Seconds' office at 1-831- 763-1800 or via www.6seconds.org.

When I decided to write this book I went to my good friend Susan Sweeney for guidance. Susan has written eight best sellers and gave generously of her time and energy to coach me. I depended on her wise counsel and without her help the book wouldn't have been written. From the bottom of my heart Susan, thank you for being such a great friend and brilliant mentor.

My friend and editor Josh Freedman was compassionately honest with me from the start. When I first sent him my book he turned me down but took the time to let me know why and what needed to be done. After I quit whimpering, I went back to work and rewrote it. After the 10th (or was it the 20th edit?) he accepted it for Six Seconds Publishing. The work we did together has made TRUSTED a book that I'm proud of and I'm so happy that it is being published by a company I trust completely. To use Bruna Martunizzi's term, you're a real Mensch.

To all of you who read my first drafts and provided valuable feedback I am in your debt. I owe each of you a big thanks. Stephanie Staples, you are an inspiration and positive role model for people who want to lead a better life... a life unlimited. Thanks for your bright light and encouragement. Michele Cederberg, it was great having you as part of the master mind group when we were all struggling to find our writing groove.

Janice Goodine, we've been best buddies now for over 40 years. You show me that kindness, integrity, perseverance and talent can take you anywhere! Chuck Wolfe, your generosity is so appreciated. Your emotions roadmap is a valuable tool and I hope this book introduces it to more people. Brent Darnell, thanks for your encouragement along the way and especially for your continuing support. You are a doer who helps others do. Kate Cannon, your wisdom and knowledge of Emotional Intelligence has guided me for many years. Dr. Jeannie Cockell, you never cease to inspire and uplift me with your positive and appreciative attitude towards life. Dr. Joan MacArthur-Blair, you put value into every day and your brilliance and tact were appreciated. Tammy Isa, my dear friend, your insights were invaluable and helped me to sculpt the book. Paula Morand, thank you for reading my first draft and for being so encouraging. Dr. Pam Robertson, your discerning eye to detail made the book better. Thank you. To my friend Louise Burley, you pushed, cajoled and prodded me to get this book written. Your enthusiasm for life and your friendship are precious jewels. Christine Taylor, it takes brilliance to make humor appear so effortless. Thank you for your brilliance.

To my children, Acacia and Phillip, you have made me a better person. You are loved beyond any cliché ever written in facebook!

My parents Harry and Ileen Birkett taught me that trust, integrity and honesty were values that are important in life. My Dad believed that a man's handshake was a contract, and he lived a life that gave all of his children an example to follow.

Most of all, I can't imagine where I would be without my husband and best friend Ric. You have believed in me when I didn't believe in myself. I love you, past, present and future.

ABOUT THE PUBLISHER

Six Seconds is a global organization supporting people to create positive change - everywhere, all the time.

We teach people how to use emotional intelligence (EQ) as the "missing link" to create breakthrough performance. Our vision is that by 2039, 1 billion people will be practicing the skills of EQ.

Utilizing powerful models and tools based in current neuroscience, Six Seconds' consultants and trainers are people-experts supporting businesses, government agencies, nonprofits, schools, and families to thrive. Six Seconds is a global network with offices in ten countries and certified practitioners in over 100 nations, all committed to being change leaders – starting from the inside.

Learn more about Six Seconds online:

www.6seconds.org

To see Six Seconds' other publications:

www.6seconds.org/tools